ON THE BAG

Seventy Years Remembered By
Pinehurst's Hall-of-Fame Caddie

WILLIE McRAE

ON THE BAG

Seventy Years Remembered By
Pinehurst's Hall-of-Fame Caddie

WILLIE McRAE

As Told to
ROB & PATTY TAFT

Published By

STEVENS PUBLISHING

Publisher's Note:
This is the second printing.

© 2014 Rob and Patty Taft

Inside photographs © Pinehurst Archives and Patty Taft

ISBN: 978-0-9912997-0-6

Published By

 STEVENS PUBLISHING COMPANY, INC.
Cincinnati, OH
info@stevenspublishingcompany.com
www.stevenspublishingcompany.com

COVER PHOTO GRAPHICS by Patty Taft of PHOTO-GRAPHICS, Pinehurst, North Carolina
Cover design: Kris Miller of KT Design, LLC, Apex, North Carolina
Book layout and typography: Stephanie Ward of TeleSet, Inc., Hillsborough, New Jersey

PRINTED IN THE UNITED STATES OF AMERICA

I would like to dedicate this book

to my ever growing family

and the wonderful people of Pinehurst.

CONTENTS

ACKNOWLEDGEMENTS

The following memoir has made me stretch my mind a long ways back. I owe a big debt of gratitude to several great people for making this book possible, especially Don Padgett and Johnny Harris and, of course, John Wolfangel, my long-time friend and publisher. I want to thank Rob Taft for pushing me to tell my story and his wife Patty for helping me say what I had to say my way. Also I appreciate the members of the Pinehurst Library and Archives for allowing us to use so many great old pictures. Let me give a special thanks to Kay Lund for helping me down Memory Lane and keeping me as straight as possible on some of my recollections...a mighty big task indeed. Please keep in mind that I've tried as best I could to tell the stories here as accurate as I know how. Some of the dates and places may be a little off, but I've tried to be true to the names and gist of the conversations. Lastly I owe a special thanks to Kris Miller for making a good looking dust jacket and Stephanie Ward for her splendid layout.

FOREWORD

*T*hese days when I look out over most of the golf courses I play, I view a sea of golf carts from the first to the eighteenth hole and find myself thinking about how golf used to be played...how it was meant to be played...a golfer with a caddie on the bag. It warms my heart to know that fine tradition still thrives on Pinehurst Number 2. Just as Donald Ross disallowed paved paths around the course so the ball could be played wherever it lay, golf carts are not allowed to crisscross the fairways of the architect's masterpiece. Oh, you can take a cart on Number 2, but you need to keep it on the unobtrusive paths. Nonetheless, taking a caddie still is the best way to get around that hallowed track.

And if you're lucky enough, you might even get Willie McRae on your bag. You'd be lucky all right but not simply because Willie reads the greens on Number 2 better than anyone or because he can choose the right club at the right time for a player he's seen swing a club only once or twice. No...they're both perfectly good reasons...but they're not the most important one. No...you'd be lucky because quite simply after seventy years of caddying experience, this gentleman personifies the history of Pinehurst itself. And you just can't do better than that.

Like its sister course, St Andrews in Scotland, known as the home of golf, Pinehurst is referred to as the home of golf here in America. Willie encapsulates the history and tradition of this fine sport at Pinehurst. I've had the pleasure of knowing Willie for many years. No golfer ever remains a stranger around Willie for very long because he has an innate sense for knowing what puts a person at ease and that rare talent of making his job a personal experience for the golfer.

Pinehurst has been fortunate to have a person such as Willie through the years. His recollections in this book are the threads that connect the generations from Donald Ross and Richard Tufts to U.S. Presidents, Bobby Jones to modern greats. It's a very special journey which truly makes this book a unique experience.

I sincerely hope you enjoy your read. I did.

Robert H. Dedman, Jr.
Chief Executive Officer

Pinehurst Resort & Country Club

FROM THE PUBLISHER

*M*y relationship with Willie, like many others, began on my first golf trip to Pinehurst. He was assigned to caddie in my group of golf buddies, and over the course of that first day, we learned of his long relationship with the fabled resort.

It was clear, early in the round that Willie was in charge. His knowledge of the Number 4 course, his green reads, club selections and stories made for one of the finest days ever spent playing this great game.

At the end of the day I asked him if we could reserve the same caddies for the rest of our stay and he gladly said, "No problem, we'll be here in the mornin' – ready to go."

From that day on, I have never visited Pinehurst when Willie wasn't in my group. It's been almost 20 years now and I am honored that he thought of me to publish this book, his story. And, I am so grateful to Rob and Patty Taft, the writers, for their diligence and countless hours of work bringing Willie's memories to life.

Willie and I have had many days together now, on all the Pinehurst courses, and each visit brings back old memories and begins new ones. I, and many others, have become much better golfers because of Willie's company.

In my opinion, he has lived one of the richest and most fulfilling lives I could imagine – a great American gentleman who has a positive influence on everyone who has ever had, or will have, the pleasure of knowing him. For a traditional golfer who prefers to play the game as it was meant to be played, by walking the course, Willie becomes your best friend. Always giving, sharing and certainly one of the best caddies America has ever known.

John Wolfangel
Stevens Publishing

BEN D. CRENSHAW

February 6, 2013

re: Willie McRae

I am happy to write a few words about my friend Willie McRae. Willie is still a big part of Pinehurst and its legacy. Here is a man who has devoted his life to the Resort.

I suppose Willie has seen more golf shots played at Pinehurst than anyone – some right and some wrong. Caddies possess an extraordinary knowledge of the game and its players, and by word of mouth, each caddie develops his own reputation. In this sense, Willie was always highly sought after by so many fine players who played Pinehurst and returned there. Great players such as Jack Burke, Jr., Tommy Bolt, Gene Sarazen and Julius Boros – just to name a few – specifically asked for Willie's expertise. That these wonderful players sought out Willie is high praise indeed.

May Willie's legacy, and his co-workers' memory continue to live on at Pinehurst.

Ben Crenshaw

Willie with the Pinehurst Putter Boy

CHAPTER ONE

GETTING STARTED

*T**he** ballroom of the New Beginning's Coliseum in Charlotte, North Carolina is big — that kinda take-your-breath-away big. Tonight it's filled with the top brass of Charlotte industry. For most men like me, born and raised your basic southern country boy, the experience might prove overwhelming, but I been rubbing elbows with the likes of these men for most of my life now, so frankly, with this tie around my neck and the suit that's hanging off the rest of me, I fit right in.*

Who am I? I'm Willie Lee McRae. I been a caddie at the Pinehurst Resort in North Carolina for almost seventy years now. That's right...seventy years and nearly a lifetime of toting bags for some of the biggest names in America...and been lucky enough to do it on a golf course so hallowed it's called the St. Andrews of the United States. Imagine that...

*Time to time, like tonight, the resort asks me to come to Charlotte to promote what they like to call the "Pinehurst Experience"...and it **is** an experience. Not just 'cause of Number 2, or the seven other golf courses, but 'cause of the entire town. Pinehurst's that bit of crisp New England style plunked down* *smack in the middle of lush southern landscape far away from cities and massive crowds. It draws and downright woos the visitor with its peaceful calm and pine-fresh air...and for lucky people like me...it's home.*

I look around and see a bunch of suits all standing around John Harris, the prominent Charlotte businessman I've caddied for a time or two. I walk on over and right away John says, "Join us," and starts introducing me to his colleagues. Seem like nice group of gents...I smile and greet each one.

"All right, Willie McRae," pipes up one of the group, "We know why you're here. So tell me, why should I go to Pinehurst?"

The in-your-face tone of his question kinda surprises me so I hesitate. "Well," I respond after thinking on it, "People there are so nice you think you're in the wrong place."

They all laugh, but now retired North Carolina Governor, James Martin, he pushes for more. "Very good, but, Willie, give us some particulars."

My head reels with memories...so many memories...more than seventy years' worth. Where do I start?

How about at the beginning? Born on the 19th of the fifth month, 1933, I was the third of twelve children. My parents, Emma Lee and Thaddeus Herman McRae, sure had their hands full with us. There were so many of us that the oldest one, my sister Magaline, was sent to New York City so my Aunt Maggie Bell could raise her. Now Lord knows I love all my brothers and sisters...truly do...we're just that kind of family. But when Magaline left, I was relieved it

Willie's Grandparents, Richmond and Lizzie Rogers

wasn't Mollie Mae they sent up north. I always had a particular attachment to Mollie Mae...you know...a special kind of bond. Her and me always been like two-peas-in-a-pod. She was the one who knew how to cool that hot temper of mine...taught me how to put the velvet on the hammer, you might say. Mollie Mae was a right

One of Willie's sisters, Mrs. Mollie Mae (McRae) Garaway.

clever girl...had to be with me...We always walked to school together too. I still remember when we trudged that whole long mile in the snow...darn cold too...only to get there and learn school was closed that day. No matter...school just ran until noon anyway so kids could go help with chores. Of course, lotta boys got bused over to Pinehurst to caddie.

Willie remembers his school days.

Anyway, Mom, Dad and the rest of us — four girls and eight boys — lived in a four-room house in Taylortown, a kinda suburb of Pinehurst. Taylortown was founded by Nicodemus Taylor. Nicodemus was an ex-slave and the first real worker at Pinehurst clubhouse. Mom always told us to follow his example 'cause he worked real hard and saved his money. By turn of the twentieth century Nicodemus had saved enough to buy a sizeable chunk of land. That land officially became known as Taylortown in 1987. But it was his son, Robert, who actually *made* Taylortown. Just like his dad, Robert was a hard worker. He ran a school for African-Americans...went right on through to the twelfth grade too. Even early on the town was comfortable...had a simple layout with couple of stores, two cafés, a barbershop and, of course, the Galilee Baptist Church.

Now my mom shared a farm with my grandparents. It had everything – tobacco, corn, tomatoes, watermelons, even cotton. If I live to be a hundred, I'll never know how she handled that farm and managed to raise so many kids too, but she did. But I'll tell you she was one of them people, when she walked into a room you just froze and stopped whatever you were doing. No questions, you just *stopped*...especially when she gave that *look*. She'd sharpen us up right quick and all she had to do was *look*. Of course, other times she'd just smile and toss out a gentle reminder...funny how she always knew when to use what...remarkable woman, truly remarkable...Mom now enjoys her 99 grandkids along with 129 great grandkids. We all celebrate her birthday every year. We gather in the sprawling front yard of the farm under our great *Tree of Knowledge*...that's our big old pecan. I smile when I think how many secrets that old tree has kept through all these years...must have a sizeable bundle of them by now I expect. Anyway, it's always a big day, Mom's birthday. Bet we have over three hundred folks come bearing gifts. I'm happy for Mom...Lord knows she's sure earned it. She deserves all that love and respect. Just shows how much love

Willie under the McRae Family's Tree of Knowledge.

she has to give too...but she still knows how to give that look!

Now eleven kids was like a built-in labor force so we each had a job to do around the farm. Before I even reached double digits, I was helping Grandpa saw down pine trees for the Pinehurst mill.

He'd put me at the tail end of the saw and tell me, "Steady, Son. You have to keep the saw steady as we go." He taught me so much...was real good to me that man. I truly loved him. So when he talked to me not like just a kid but more like a person worth his time, I'd focus even harder on that crosscut saw. I'd study that blade so hard that after awhile I didn't even notice the rich scent of the pine coming off that fresh cut wood. No...was just that blade in front of me and my grandpa's words in my head.

Mom and Dad was real busy with all the other kids, so I was lucky to have my grandparents close by 'cause they had more time to spend with me. They taught me a lot. I think most of what I learned of the world I got from them. They raised me like my aunt in New York raised my older sister Magaline. After school I would help Grandpa with chores. So I managed to stay out of trouble for that portion of the day...but going to and from school I did my share of fighting. Grandpa mighta been telling me to keep the saw steady, but Grandma always was studying my face and arms for new bruises...I had a *bunch*...and after awhile I couldn't hide them no more.

"Fighting," she scolded. "Don't do that, Willie! Turn the cheek."

"What am I supposed to *do*?" I'd complain when she started in that way. "Don't *like* turning the cheek."

She'd smile. Grandma always spoke her mind but never raised

her voice. Of course she still took that paddle to me more than once. You know it takes years to learn when to discipline one way and when to use the other...and I think some people never do get it right. But she was a pro at it. "You allow yourself to get into fights every day," she'd say. "And most of them are over nothing much. Am I right?"

Of course she was right and that look I'd always give her just fueled the fire and urged her on. "Then you're fighting 'cause you're proud and that's not reason enough."

At first I tried to argue, but it never did any good...never won...she was way smarter than her wise-ass, hard-headed grandson.

"You can't fight *everyone*, Willie," she said. "You fighting over *everything* means you're always right and the other guy's always wrong. *You that smart?*"

I wasn't. She knew I wasn't...hell...*I* knew I wasn't.

"Learn to keep your mouth shut and move on," she warned, " 'cause some things are worth fighting for and some things aren't. The big things...*they're* worth fighting for. You need to save your energy for *them*!"

Would be years before all her lessons sank in, but when they did, they took for life. Years later when I was in the army, I wrote her a letter. In it I thanked her for keeping me out of jail because I knew that's where I woulda been if it hadn't been for her. Now she never told *me*, but I heard from more than one of the family how that letter tickled her but good. That letter was small payment for all she did for me and I wanted her to know all her patience with me had been worth her time...that her attention hadn't been wasted on me.

The people who really care about you need to know that...and you
need to tell them.

Now we lived mostly off money that came from the farm's tobacco
and cotton, along with mill money from the pine wood. Grew most
our food too but you still had to know how to cook it...and that was
my mom's department. Mom was in charge of all the cooking and
teaching my sisters how to work a kitchen. My mouth still waters
every time I remember my mom's chicken and rice. Her gravy
smelled so good it seemed to just reach out and draw you to the
table...made you feel the growling in your belly. But dad kept us all
in line...well...when he was sober anyway.

"We'll wait to be served, now won't we?" he'd say, sternly
eyeballing each one of us. His question wasn't a question at all – it
was a warning. We knew if he had to repeat it, there'd be
trouble...*big* trouble.

Now Mom was a regular church-goer...but more than that she was
a true Christian in her spirit and it showed in her generosity. We
always grew way more than even our big family could eat so Mom
would have us bag and give what we didn't need to neighbors. They
loved her for that kindness – never forgot it neither. So of course
since Mom was a regular church-goer, so was all us kids. Every
Sunday come hell or high water she hauled every one of us off to
Galilee Baptist Church. Had to be down with fever or curled around
the toilet bowl before we could get out of Sunday church. Then come
night the girls would scramble into bunk beds in one room, and
Mom and Dad would go to their room. My seven brothers and me
would just sprawl out in cots or on thin mattresses on the living

Willie in front of Galilee Baptist Church

room floor. We'd all chatter a while, then fall asleep.

One night...I was about ten...Dad stormed from his room. "I want quiet in here!" he bellowed. "Idle chatter at bedtime's a sign that you're not working enough during the day!"

Silence fell hard like a hammer and ruled the room.

Come morning, Dad took me outside where we'd be alone. I remember the deliberate way he moved frightened me. When we reached our *Tree of Knowledge,* he said, "Sit, Son."

I obeyed without thinking or breathing and kept my eyes glued on him.

He gazed at me. I could smell the alcohol from the night before still on his breath. "It's time you got to work," he announced.

"But I already help Grandpa with cutting wood," I defended. "I wasn't talking last night, I swear."

He shot me a look that told me he knew I was lying, but he let the fib slide. "I know, Son," he said. "But there's a war on and we need you to do more."

World War II was three years old with no end in sight.

"Make some money for your mother. Your mother and me been talking about it. It's time."

There was no sense arguing. "But what am I gonna *do*?"

"Follow in my footsteps," he replied. "You can be a caddie like me."

Although he worked regular at Carolina Pharmacy, Dad caddied at Pinehurst whenever he could. But *that* wasn't for *me*. My heart sank. I felt trapped. I tried to wiggle free, but all I could offer up was a feeble, "But I don't know nothin' about caddying."

Dad just smiled his knowing wry smile. "Then it's time you learned. Caddying is a way of life for most of us in Taylortown. Besides, I know everything you need to know. I'll teach you"

"I'm only *ten*."

"Old enough to lug a flower sack or two," he smiled back at me and already I could feel myself weighted down carrying flimsy old golf bags.

My face was still twisted in a knot when dad picked up an old garbage bag and a small, dead branch that had fallen from our *Tree of Knowledge*. He stood the bag up best he could and stuffed the limb into it. "Pretend this here's a golf bag and this branch a club. When the player approaches you, stand the bag up. Hold it still but back up a step." He held the bag at arms-length as I stared blank-like at the branch and limp bag. "Let him see *all* the clubs. Got it?"

I nodded all sullen and unhappy.

"Good," he said. "Now they'll ask you what club they should use for different shots. When I take you up to the course, I'll show you a complete set of clubs and go over each one with you."

"How many are there?"

"There's 14...no more," he replied. "If a player has more than that he's cheating."

"But how I'm gonna learn about 14 clubs and know which one to give for each shot?"

Dad didn't have an easy answer for *that* one. "You'll figure it out."

That didn't help much...and dad knew it.

"Listen," he said. "You watch a player hit a few shots with different clubs and you'll see how far he hits each one. He might hit a 1-wood 200 yards or just 150. He might hit a 5-iron a hundred." He shrugged. "Or...125."

The more he tried to explain, the more the whole nasty mess sounded like Greek.

"It'll come, Son," he said at length. "Give it time. In the meantime the important thing is to...*show up, keep up and shut up.*"

When Dad makes up his mind about something he wastes no time, so he dragged me down to the resort after school that very same day to meet the caddie master, Jack Williams. There were several golfers waiting to go so Mr. Williams was already busy. Dad no sooner told the man who I was when he said, "I need the boy on a bag *now.*"

"But he's never caddied before!"

That caddie master checked me out head-to-toe and said, "No matter," before barking more orders at two other caddies. "We'll have him following in your footsteps in no time." That comment pleased Dad into a toothpaste ad smile. Mr. Williams sized me up again and winked, "Might even make another Gaines out of him."

Ed Gaines was the model caddie from the 1920s. Oh he had what it took all right, even a big toothy grin that became the trademark of the Pinehurst caddie. Even back then there was a huge demand for caddies, so Pinehurst — Donald Ross, that is — made an arrangement with the school in Taylortown to send over their older boys. Good reliable caddies were real hard to come by at first. Worse still, the good pay — a quarter for the first hour and a nickel for every 20 minutes after that — attracted a bad element. Rough older guys intimidated the golfers. Why, it got so bad, Mr. Ross thought about bringing in black *girls* as caddies. But then he hired Donald Currie. Currie cleaned up the problem and then bragged that he'd made a crew of top-notch "happy" caddies. That was the group Jack Williams inherited in the mid-30's.

Pinehurst caddies at that time were a lot different from Northern caddies. Back then your Northern caddies, well they were mainly teenage white boys — kids doing a job for some summer, spending money and waiting on school to start up again. But Pinehurst caddies were more serious. Had to be 'cause for many of them, caddying would be their lives — how they got by — what they had to look forward to. Of course, they had that reputation of Ed Gaines

Caddies On The Rail

to live up to, too. So Pinehurst caddies, well...they always made sure they showed ear-to-ear smiles. Heck some even wore names of famous Americans on their uniforms...names like Teddy Roosevelt and Jesse James. Believe that?

Now it was my turn like it or not to become part of that group. My heart was pounding. Was I *ready*? How could *anyone* think *I* was ready for *this*? I sure didn't feel ready. Felt like someone was shoving me off a cliff and all the while smiling back at me just waiting on the big splat that comes at the bottom.

"I'll put him with Hardrock Robinson," Mr. Williams said. Guess since Hardrock was such an experienced caddie, he felt this would be a safe move. He looked me over once more and shook his head. "You'll do fine, kid."

Next thing I know the caddie master pointed to a flour sack and told me to pick it up. "Put the strap over your shoulder," Mr. Williams instructed, "and get your butt out there." Looking back those bags were small, but full of clubs like they were, they weighed me down pretty good. I was already late so I made out for the 1st tee fast as I could. Looking on up ahead I saw Hardrock and three golfers all kinda scowlie-faced and impatient looking, dressed in knickerbockers. I fumbled my way toward them. I felt off balance...awkward...at a real disadvantage...and I was *mad*. Right then I hated Dad for getting me into this mess...and I hated the caddie master just for being part of it all. And truth be told I didn't care much for them guys on the tee, neither. Why couldn't I do something *else*? Why'd I have to *caddy?*

I got to the tee and remembered what Dad had said. Well...I'd showed up. Now I all I had to do was shut up and try my best to keep up. I caddied for Jimmy Hunter that first day. He eyeballed me, studied me up and down like I was some kinda insect, and then greeted me coolly with a grunt and a snort. I stood gaping at him, his bag still on my shoulder. All I was thinking about was how long this afternoon was gonna be. Could I be *this* tired so *soon* or was I just this *nervous*? I'd already forgotten Dad's other rule: put the bag down, step back...didn't remember it until Mr. Hunter asked, "Can I have my club?" I promptly set the bag down in response. He chose the longest club in his bag. Still irritated, he set up the ball and smacked it square down the fairway.

As we took off, Hardrock whispered, "The club your player hit was a driver."

"I *know* that."

"Then give it to him on every tee, but not on the par 3s."

I nodded. Dad had already explained more than that. I was smarter than Hardrock gave me credit, but I guess it was his job to start me at the beginning.

"Where's your towel," he snapped.

Towel? Was he serious? Dad never said nothing about no towel.

"You need to clean off the club after the man hits."

That was news to me.

"You'll have to use mine," he said full of genuine disgust.

Now I hadn't seen Mr. Hunter hit except for his drive so I didn't know how to club him. Setting down the bag, stepping back and letting him choose a club got me by the first few holes. Hardrock was quick to oblige when the golfers asked for help reading the greens, so I thought things were going pretty good...even started to kinda like what I was doing...started thinking maybe I really *could* take to this caddying. But my honeymoon braked real sudden on the 5th hole, the second of back-to-back par 5s.

That good feeling I'd just started to get happy about drained from my body real fast in the middle of the fifth fairway when Mr. Hunter snapped, "Give me the spoon."

I froze. *The spoon?* Was he joking me?

"Don't have a spoon, suh," I replied honestly. I peered one-eyed, deep into his bag. "And don't see one in your bag neither."

He scowled at me. *"Are you serious, kid?"*

Hardrock kicked me subtly from behind as Mr. Hunter measured my inexperience. But the man suddenly smiled...then he downright belly laughed. "Hah," he hollered. "The 3-wood then. The spoon is the 3-wood." He was calm and still smiling. "Willie, what do you say I teach you the clubs?" And right there on the 5th fairway with a group of golfers waiting behind us, Mr. Hunter taught me about all the clubs in his bag from the *brassie* — 2-wood — to the *mashie* — 9-iron.

I was just ten, but I knew Mr. Hunter wasn't laughing at me...was more like the situation tickled him. No, he was helping me. So instead of sassing him, like my ten-year-old-usual-wise-ass self woulda done, I hung on his every word. If I was gonna be a caddie, I needed to learn everything — and *fast*. By the 14th hole I really thought I had the roll of the greens. But the read I gave Mr. Hunter for *that* green couldn'ta been more wrong. What I'd seen as an obvious break to the right broke left instead. My golfer left the green disgruntled. Hardrock caught me by the sleeve just as I hoisted the flower sack back on my shoulder and hissed like an angry snake.

"Which way does the sun come up?" His face was all full of disapproval and he sounded downright *mad*.

"What?"

"Which way does the sun come up?" he hissed again.

"East," I answered.

"Good. You know *that* much anyway," he said. "The grass always grows to the sun."

"So?"

"*So,*" he replied, irritated at my snot-nosed kid tone, "the ball always breaks east to west. Remember that and maybe, just maybe, you'll learn to read greens."

Hardrock and me didn't say much after that. I thought he was still pretty mad but then coming up to the 18th hole he surprised me by saying, "Kid, you've got a good attitude for this. I think you're gonna make it."

I remember his words to this day. You know, he didn't have to say that, but he did...and at exactly the right time, too, 'cause before he told me that I'd done nothing but worry from the 15th tee to just before that 18th hole. Didn't think I could make it as a caddie. By the time the clubhouse came into view and we were trekking up to the 18th hole, I'd come up with a whole bunch of excuses for Dad for why I couldn't caddie. Guess Hardrock saw the worry written on my face 'cause his words nailed it like a cork plugs a dam. Even Mr. Hunter (who I was calling 'Jimmy' by third or fourth time I caddied for him) ended the round on a high note. "You like caddying, Willie?" he asked as he handed me $1.25, which included a tip.

I smiled, maybe just a little too big, and answered, "Yes, suh, I do."

"Well, I like you as a caddie," he replied and invited me to shag balls for him the next Thursday.

Funny how just a few simple words of encouragement can turn things around. You know, to this day I still don't know why more people don't realize just a few kind words can make all the difference. I felt on top of the world when we left the course...the long walk back to Taylortown would go easy that night. Little did I know I still had another surprise coming.

As we made our way back to the clubhouse, Hardrock put his arm around me and said, "Now we dance." I had no idea what he was talking about but as we rounded the clubhouse to the large practice putting green, I could tell something big was about to happen 'cause when we came into view a crowd began congregating. Some golfers left the putting green, others got up from their tables. They all formed a horseshoe at the foot of the steps around a big tub where another caddie, Robert Stafford, was sitting with a washboard between his knees. He handed Hardrock a pair of shoes. Hardrock took them but before he'd even put them on the crowd began to cheer. Hardrock bowed wearing a grin so big it coulda lit up a ballroom.

What followed I'll *never* forget. Hardrock took to the pavement clicking and clacking while Robert played that washboard. I just stood there, my slack low hanging jaw making me look simple, while this man who'd lugged two flower sacks for 18 holes now tapped with a child's energy. Later came to learn before he'd been caddying, Hardrock had been a top-notch tap dancer and entertainer...used to perform on stage. Why he took to caddying I'll never know. But while Hardrock was a great caddie, watching him then I think he was an even better tap dancer. His feet moved so fast...with such rhythm...only a man born to dance coulda done it. I wondered how his legs could muster the strength to make those moves...*incredible* moves. The faster he tapped, the louder the cheering got...and the

After Golf Entertainment compliments of Pinehurst Caddies

louder the cheering got, the more money poured into the tub. It was just at that moment I saw...no...more like I understood. Hardrock didn't just *dance,* he drew the crowd right *into* his tapping and made them part of it. The excitement of that magical unspoken communication sent a charge like electricity right through the crowd and through the late afternoon air...was almost like he couldn't succeed *without* them cheering. Hardrock shared his talent and the crowd shared their excitement. And while I watched the excitement of the guests and club members become one with Hardrock's tapping, I realized Hardrock had just taught me another lesson about caddying...a lesson I wish I'd thanked him for but sad enough never did. Right then I came to see the bigger picture. Golf's a game all right, but a game's just entertainment and true entertainment is all about give and take. Now I figure since communication done right is a two-way street...so the way I see it, if I appreciate someone, he'll appreciate *me* back. That very important piece of insight is thanks to Hardrock and from that day to now, I always been mindful of it when I caddy.

When the dancing was finished, and the crowd scattered slow into the twilight, Hardrock scooped up the money from the tub.

"What about *me*?" Robert demanded.

Hardrock broke into that grin again. "When they come to see *you*," he said, "*then* the money's yours."

I thought about what he said as I hoofed it home that night. Yeah, kinda seemed unfair of Hardrock about the money and I wasn't real sure it fit the lesson I just come away with...never did quite settle it in my mind neither. Still the excitement of the whole day made the long walk home seem shorter, and that night I fell asleep happy knowing I got to do it all over again the next day.

Willie takes a moment to remember his childhood mentors Donald J. Ross (L) and Richard Tufts (R).

CHAPTER TWO

RICHARD TUFTS, DONALD ROSS AND A NEW PAIR OF SHOES

"*So from that day on I was a caddie.*" *The cluster of men around me had grown some while I was telling my story. They musta gotten a kick out of my start. I hadn't planned on telling that story and am real surprised how smooth and kinda easy it all came to me. They press me for more...Well I figure I'm here for them...so what do they want to know?*

"Do they really have eight golf courses at Pinehurst?" asks one man. He's wearing a pinstriped navy blue suit with a powder blue shirt and green tie. I look around again. For sure too many names to keep straight...guess I'll just tag them by tie color and not worry about names.

"Yes indeed," I tell him. "Five surrounding the main club house, and three off-site."

The man shakes his head. "Why so many?"

I smile. "It's Pinehurst."

More questions just keep coming. Did a doctor really build the first course? Does Ben Crenshaw prefer the greens on Number 3? Is Number 4 the most beautiful? Number 7 the hardest?

I raise my hands and ask for forgiveness. "Gentleman, I wasn't around when it all started, but I'm gonna try my best here. Golf-wise, Pinehurst started with a 9-hole course. Just over 2,500 yards from the 1st tee to the last green, all sixty acres of her. Back in the 1890s James Tufts came here and started up the village for health reasons. It was just around the time golf was coming to America. After seeing people whacking golf balls around cow fields, he thought maybe the game would be good exercise. So he asked Dr. Leroy Culver to design him a golf course 'cause the good doctor had been to the Old Course, St. Andrews. Now Dr. Culver believed a course should be flat, shouldn't have a lot of bunkers or other obstacles. So that's how he laid out the first course."

"What were the tees like back then?" asks the man in a red tie.

"Built up a little bit, but small," I tell him. "Enough to stand on and that's about it."

"And the greens?" asks someone in a red and black tie.

"They were flat too...sixty-feet by sixty-feet square," I say. "They rolled the areas around the greens. The greens were made of clay and sand you know?"

Most don't. The man wearing a beige tie asks, "Why no grass?"

"Too hard to grow and keep like the grass today," I answer. "But they would smooth the greens over with big swaths of carpet. People putted them okay, I guess."

"What did Donald Ross think about Course Number 1?" asks a man sporting a brown paisley tie.

"Not much. Didn't matter what the doctor said, Mr. Ross didn't think the course resembled St Andrews very much."

"Did he fix it?" asks red tie.

"Sure did," I tell them. "You see, Mr. Ross knew how to build sand traps. Knew how to make greens that drained the water right, too. That let him elevate them some. You know, turn Mother Nature upside down and plant a few elephants in them."

They chuckled over that description until green tie remarked, "That's a shame. I hear Ross greens are infamously cruel."

"They are a challenge," another adds. "But that's his signature."

"And Number 2?" asks brown paisley.

My eyebrows arch. "That was his prize."

"How long did it take him to build?"

"Most of fifty years," I answer. "If he was with us now, he'd still be fooling with it."

"Did you ever get to caddie for him?" asks a man in a polka-dotted yellow tie.

I smile as another story starts to come together in my head. I nod. "Him and Richard Tufts both."

There's been a lot said and I expect even more written about the history of Pinehurst so I won't bother you with it too much. I expect it's enough to say James Walker Tufts, the man who developed Pinehurst, was a very rich man...a smart man from Massachusetts. Now he had figured out how to grow his wealth by combining his pharmacies with a new-fangled thing called the soda fountain. Not a man in the best of health, Mr. Tufts heard about the health benefits of the North Carolina Sandhills – clean air, moderate climate – and decided that's where he needed to live. So he sold off all his businesses, bought property from local landowners and put together a huge chunk of land. Oh, everyone thought he was plum crazy to do it. The Sandhills back then was pretty much a barren place. Had a few restaurants and hotels — all crude by northern standards...but not to James Tufts. This man had *vision*. He was gonna do with the Sandhills what he'd done with all his pharmacies when he brought in those soda fountains. And his dream for the Sandhills was to bring a piece of New England to the South. You can see that in the look of the village.

Now Mr. Tufts was a kind man. He wanted to spend his money doing good deeds so he founded the village to attract people just like him — people with health problems. People who needed to cure what ailed them. Big evergreens, happy to grow in the sandy soil, soaked the clean air with the scent of fresh pine just made Pinehurst that much more attractive. You know when you take a good, deep breath of something that fresh and clean, well, you just feel better for it.

But when Mr. Tufts and his son Leonard built Pinehurst, they never forgot the contribution African Americans had made here. The Tufts all treated us well. They worked to create what didn't seem to exist elsewhere — a place of goodwill and fairness. Prominent northerners wanting all types of sport flocked to visit here. They discovered our culture and it intrigued them...always brought them back, time and time again.

Pinehurst thrived right on through the 1920s. Came to be known as the Cup Capital — was a real tournament destination ever since Leonard Tufts started holding tournaments here in the early 1900s.

There was the Sterling Silver Cup on Thanksgiving Day, the Casino Cup, the Christmas Cup, the Holly Inn Cup and, of course, the annual North South tournaments. The only tournament that didn't have a cup in the early days was the Pinehurst Club Championship, funny, huh? Still a big deal though. But like with so many things back then, the Great Depression, along with World War II, crushed the spirited life of the '20s. By the '30s, all that was pretty much just a memory. Pinehurst couldn't escape what was happening any more than any other place could. Even though the resort hosted the PGA Tournament in 1936 and began the Caddie Tournament three years later, there was a certain uneasiness cutting through the place when I came on the scene.

Believe it or not, German POWs ended up in the Sandhills 'cause the army put them to work picking peaches in the orchards. And even way out in the middle of nowhere — or close to it — people found themselves living under blackout rules and practicing air-raid drills. In the two years before I started caddying, over 500 military officers had come and gone through Pinehurst. They took over the Carolina Hotel and punctured her walls with a new collection of phone lines. Yes, even our Carolina had her war wounds — shoulda at least given her a Purple Heart for everything she put up with. And once the army took over, they decided golf was just a frivolous game. The Office of Price Administration cut back on how many golf balls could be manufactured and word had it that even Richard Tufts said that Pinehurst "operated from hand-to-mouth." A war that big...don't matter *where* you are...isn't anyone or anything ever safe from it.

"Would they really drop bombs down here?"

I managed to land my question smack in the middle of my dad's latest lecture to me and he barked back, "Son, we're not talking about the war. Now listen to me. You got a tongue on you that needs controlling. Just because you *thought* that golfer yesterday was too proud, don't mean you *say* it. You keep your mouth shut. Hear me? No sass!"

I nodded. I wasn't gonna say a word. I knew better than to argue with Dad when he got like this. He was just about crazy mad.

He took me hard by the shoulders. I felt so small in his burly grip. Felt like crying but was afraid to. "Look, Son, the idea out there is to make money — money to help your mom. All of us, right? You wanna do that, right?"

I could hardly breathe so I nodded.

"Good. But to do that you're gonna have to be *professional*," he went on. "And you're professional when you keep the man happy."

After that, Mom took me aside. "Listen to him, Willie. He's just trying to make you right. Make you the best caddie you can be."

"Mom, I'll try," I told her. "But I can't be the best caddie with these shoes. They hurt my feet."

"We've talked about this," she said, her tone stern. "Times now are tough, even with those food vouchers from Mr. Tufts."

"But I don't know how much longer I can go in these old things." I looked down at the mean old culprits and scuffed my feet with sullen purpose.

She straightened and eyeballed me. "I hope you're not thinking what I think you're thinking."

Of course I was. She knew me like a book.

"I don't want you asking Mr. Tufts for no more favors," she said. "Am I making myself clear?"

"Perfectly," I thought, but that's not what I said. "But he's a nice man, Mom."

"That doesn't mean you can be asking him for shoes," she replied. "He's got his own troubles. It's a bad time for everybody, even him."

"But I can't keep putting cardboard in my shoes," I argued. "It doesn't *last.*"

Poor Mom — she took that remark personally. I didn't mean for her to, but I could see the weight of poor business and a large family on her shoulders. "I'll ask nice, Mom. I really will."

She peered down at me with sad eyes, said nothing, then turned and left the room. Well it wasn't exactly a *yes,* but I figured it wasn't a *no* either. Now I knew my parents were right, but I really needed new shoes and the way I saw it, Mr. Tufts was the only man in Pinehurst who could help me out.

On our way to school the next day, my feet started hurting real bad. I thought I could get some sympathy from Mollie Mae, but when I complained she reacted like Mom and Dad rolled into one. I remember she ended by saying, "Live as if you like everybody, Willie, and you'll succeed in life." Mollie Mae ended all her lectures to me with that advice...guess she figured I couldn't hear it too often...she was right, too. My sister Mollie Mae was smart as anyone. She later went on to college — taught for 37 years, and then supervised that same school we used to go to for another three. I only made it through tenth grade, but she taught me much of the rest. Mollie

Mae taught me what mattered — how to be honest and get along with people, how important it was and how much of a difference it would make in my life.

Two days later I caddied for Richard Tufts and Donald Ross. I'd caddied for both men before. Knew they could flat out play, but this was the first time I got to watch them play together. The two men were so different. Mr. Tufts came from Pinehurst royalty. But now Donald Ross, he ran the golf program at Pinehurst — had been there ever since James Tufts had recruited him back in the early 1900s. Back then there was a Harvard Professor, name of Robert Wilson. He was the one who convinced Donald Ross to leave Scotland and come to America to be the pro at some country club up in Massachusetts. Then the professor introduced Mr. Ross to Mr. Tufts and the rest, like they say, is history. The two men hit it off right from the start so Mr. Ross ended up as pro and then course designer in Pinehurst. The man could do it all — design courses and maintain them, both. And *golf?* Donald Ross could play with the best of them and make it look easy. By the time I caddied for him, Mr. Ross was a Pinehurst institution.

The conversation Richard Tufts and Donald Ross had that day intrigued me right from the 1st tee of Number 2. After striping their drives some 250 yards down the middle of the fairway, the two men started up. I was there to caddie, to listen, shut up and keep up. That's it. Never thought any golfers would pay me any mind, much less these two...Mr. Tufts was worried about how the club was losing money and Mr. Ross complained that with his paltry budget — he used the word *paltry* — he was hard pressed to maintain the golf courses like he wanted. The way Mr. Tufts kept on, I decided I'd best keep my mouth shut and not ask for shoe money. So when Mr. Tufts asked me to recommend a club for his 2nd shot on the 1st hole, I just handed him a 9-iron and stepped back.

I did a good job to keep silent all the way through the 3rd fairway. When Mr. Tufts needed a 9-iron for his approach shot, I just handed it to him and stepped back again.

"Willie," he said. "What's the matter with you today?"

His question took me by surprise. Since I had decided to stay invisible I actually had started to feel that I was. "Nothing, suh," I replied.

"Why aren't you saying anything?"

"Don't know, suh," I lied. "Guess I figure you know the club you need more than me."

When we got to the green, he asked me to read his putt. *Imagine, Mr. Tufts asking me to do that when he was standing right next to Donald Ross!* Both men, especially the one who'd built this course, sure knew these greens a lot better than I did. Still surprised, I looked over the putt, determined the grain and slope, and gave my best guess. It worked. The putt trickled in, bringing a wide grin to Mr. Tufts' face. I smiled back and then found myself opening up more and more on just about every hole.

Mr. Ross was still complaining about the condition of the course, when before I even knew or could stop it, the question on my mind came spilling out of my mouth. "Have you *ever* been happy with this course?"

Both men stiffened. I shoulda kept my mouth shut. What had I done? They studied me in stony silence. But now Mr. Tufts, he actually snuck a smile. "What about that, Don?" he said turning to Mr. Ross. "Have you ever been *satisfied* with this course?"

The designer ignored the question. Instead, he replied, "No, Willie, Number 2 is actually looking better now than it used to years ago." He related how difficult it was to get grass to grow in the sandy soil and how they had clay greens until just six years earlier. "We used to roll the fairways — called them fair greens back then — but we were really rolling sand to keep them nice and tight. Even when clumps of grass actually would grow, they only managed to make the fairways look like rough. Can you believe it?"

"The grass looks okay now," I said as we walked. "How come?"

"We found a new kind of grass," he said. "We're always looking for new kinds of grass."

"Don't let him kid you, Willie," Mr. Tufts inserted. "Mr. Ross has a knack for these things. If grass won't grow, he'll find a way to grow it. And he has the best eye I've ever seen for carving a golf course out of any natural setting."

The rest of the round was like a history lesson. How Pinehurst got started, the time Francis Oiumet, the first American to win the U.S. Open, won the North South, exhibition matches featuring the great Harry Vardon...

"Could you beat him, Mr. Ross?" I just had to ask.

He smiled. "*No one* could beat Harry."

"Except Francis in that glorious U.S. Open," Mr. Tufts noted, being a proud New Englander.

"How did you come to build Number 2?" I asked.

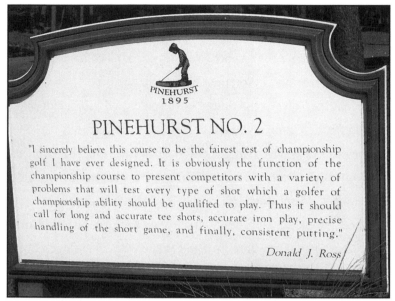

PINEHURST
1895

PINEHURST NO. 2

"I sincerely believe this course to be the fairest test of championship golf I have ever designed. It is obviously the function of the championship course to present competitors with a variety of problems that will test every type of shot which a golfer of championship ability should be qualified to play. Thus it should call for long and accurate tee shots, accurate iron play, precise handling of the short game, and finally, consistent putting."

Donald J. Ross

Donald Ross's Pledge for Number 2

"Don't get him started on that," Mr. Tufts said. "You see when he came here the only course in Pinehurst was the nine-hole version of Course 1."

"Then they tried to expand it," Mr. Ross cut in, "by adding tee boxes on six of the existing holes." He shook his head. "The original course had only one tree on it."

"Kinda like St. Andrews," I piped up again when I shouldn'ta.

An uncomfortable silence hit fast and hard. As for Donald Ross, he knifed me a look so sharp my mouth went dry. "What do *you* know about St. Andrews?"

"Not much, suh," I said, regretting the mistake I'd made. But just then I heard Mr. Tufts utter beneath his breath, "Boy's got a point."

Mr. Ross gazed into my eyes. "What I saw fell well short of why

James Tufts brought me here," he said. "After all, I came from Scotland, home of golf. And as I've told almost every American golfer I see, 'You must go to Dornoch. Now there's a place for golf.' "

"So then he says..." prompted his friend.

"I told the Tufts at the time — both senior and junior," declared Donald Ross. "I'll build you a real course."

The process proved to be easier said than done. Mr. Ross finished the front 9 of Number 2 in 1901. But with the passing of James Tufts and his son, Leonard, trying to manage the club by long-distance, it took Mr. Ross another six years to finish his prize, or at least get it to a point where he could fiddle with all eighteen holes.

We had reached the 13th hole. By now my feet were burning and pulsed with pain. As we trudged up the hill to the green, Mr. Tufts musta caught the grimace on my face.

"What's the matter, Willie?" he asked.

I could hear my folks' words in my head. "Nothing, suh," I muttered trying real hard to ignore the almost unbearable pain in my feet.

He shrugged. We kept walking. He didn't say another word to me until the 14th green. "Willie, are you sure you're all right?"

"Yes, suh," I managed.

"Are you sure? Because you don't look all right."

I didn't know what to say. "We really appreciate the food vouchers you give us."

"Why, thank you, Willie."

"They help out a lot."

He studied me for a moment. "That's nice to hear."

But something in my brain musta went haywire. That little voice that kept telling me, *Don't do it Willie Lee, ya hear? Don't you do it!* was losing out to the screaming pain in my feet. They hurt bad — real bad. Then my mouth just seemed to take over with a will of its own. "It's like we can ask you for anything. You're that nice." Great...where did *that* come from? Now I was sounding like I was blowing smoke...Dear Lord, can't *you* stop my mouth?

"Ah huh," he agreed. "I like to think that people who work for me can come to me if they need to."

"Even though the club's losing money?" I carefully asked. *Shut up, Willie, just shut up. Just STOP, now!*

He straightened. I could see he regretted having talked club finances in front of me. "What's your point, Willie?"

"I need a new pair of shoes. These hurt so bad," I blurted. No running for shelter now, I thought.

"I see," he said. We walked on in silence. He never said another word to me until the 18th hole. By then I was sure he was gonna tell Dad what I said and that scared the daylights out of me. I never shoulda opened my mouth. Keep up and shut up, that's what I shoulda done. Why couldn't I just do that? I wanted out of there real bad. Forget the shoes. Finish up that double loop and scram — that's all I wanted now.

I was so itching to flee, I barely thanked him when he paid me after the round. I started to leave but he said, "Willie, come back here." When I turned around and looked up at him, I noticed he was smiling at me the way Dad sometimes did. "If you're going to caddy here, you need a good pair of shoes. Come see me tomorrow."

The next day Mr. Tufts handed me a brand new pair of Buster Browns. That was the first of two pair he would buy me. Fine man that Mr. Tufts.

Donald Ross and Richard Tufts — two real different people but both of them fine men on and off the course. So when I recall Mr. Tufts, I think about the Carolina Hotel — that elegant, five-star testament to him and his family. But I think about those shoes too...And when I remember Donald Ross, I think about *his* hotel, the Pine Crest Inn, and how it's all casual and laid back, like the way the clubhouse was when he ran it. Each establishment fitting the way each man was — like it should be. Was nice how two men who grew up so different were able come together for something important to them. They were the right men for the time — and downright lucky for us too. Not just two great friends...and boy could they flat out play that game of golf!

Bobby Jones on his 1935 visit to celebrate
the inauguration of grass greens on Number 2.
Willie and he wouldn't meet for another 10 years.

CHAPTER THREE

THE FABULOUS
BOBBY JONES

I *look around...still haven't lost any audience. Think it's grown some instead...and those questions just keep coming.*

"Why did you say it took Donald Ross fifty years to build Number 2?" asks the man in the red tie.

"Well he never was quite happy with the course," I reply. "You know it started like Number 1 — with just nine holes."

"Really?" green tie says in disbelief.

"Yes, suh, was no more than 1,300 yards."

A chorus of "No's!" follow from the crowd.

"In those six years it took to finish the course they added a back 9." I go on, "And only one of the original holes survived."

"They changed holes?" yellow tie questions.

"Oh they're all the time changing holes," I answer. "Holes on Number 3 have found their way onto Number 5 and holes on Number 5 onto 4 and so on. Fact they closed Number 4 down for a while 'cause they thought we didn't need so many courses. Turned it into pasture for Pinehurst's prize winning herd of cattle."

"You're kidding?" I hear from someone...not sure who.

"Absolutely," I state most surely. "One hole – the one they call the Cathedral Hole – why that one's been on all five courses around the main club house except for Number 2."

Don't think anyone knows what to say to that 'cause it gets real quiet. Then I hear a chuckle from the back. "Number 2 had sand greens," he sniffed. "When did you say they got real grass?"

"It was 1935," I tell him. "And Bobby Jones played the first day they had it."

"The Great Jones?" wonders green tie. "Ever caddie for him?"

I smile. My head swims full with another memory...

I truly was blessed in my early caddying years. My relationship with Mr. Tufts and Mr. Ross gave me great opportunities – like caddying for Robert Tyre (Bobby) Jones.

I'd learned to be a good caddie. I took extra care to see just how far players hit each club, so when I handed them one, they wouldn't end up disappointed with the outcome. I used to walk all the Pinehurst greens on my own time so that I'd know how the ball would break from any point. Had to do it. That Mr. Ross – well, he liked to challenge a golfer. Now some say he was crafty, but others complain he was downright evil 'cause he liked to put in optical illusions. Putts that golfers swore would break right, turned left instead and others that *appeared* to run uphill really ran *down*. A caddie had to be able to read greens from all angles to get any putt right. Besides on a Ross course no matter how large a green is, there's only a real small area where a golfer can hit and have the ball hold. So a good caddie has to be able to read the greens, know the spine of the roll and the way the grass leans to the sun. But I didn't just want to be a *good* caddie. *No* suh! I wanted to be the *best* caddie and to caddie for the *best*.

Now Bobby Jones was a lawyer by profession. He called Atlanta home but liked to visit Pinehurst right often. He played Pinehurst Number 2 in 1935 on the very first day the course opened with grass greens. His strong relationship with Richard Tufts and his admiration for Donald Ross' unmatched course design skill, kept him coming back year after year. I enjoyed the good graces of both those men so they made sure I was around when Mr. Jones came to town.

It mighta been how he was raised or 'cause he was an attorney, but Bobby Jones always carried himself like nobility. I'd heard he'd had a temper long time ago, but when I knew him, I couldn't imagine him ever losing it. Mr. Jones was the perfect gentlemen... could dress the part, too – from his sun visor right down to his knickers and knee-socks.

It was 1945, that's when I met him. I was just fourteen when I landed on the bag of the fabulous Bobby Jones for the first time. Now the man mighta been past his prime, but I'll tell you, he still was dead-on accurate. He hit half dozen or so balls on the range and I promise you each shot was a carbon copy of the one before. The two 9-iron shots had the exact same trajectory, two 5-iron shots, the same, lower and longer, and the drives he hit...straight as arrows and *far*. He told me once that the straight shot was the hardest one to hit, but he'd mastered it just the same. When I picked up his golf balls I couldn't help but notice that the drives were some 260 yards out but all lying just a couple of feet apart from each other.

Unbelievable! Standing back on the range I saw why he was so accurate. His swing — it never varied. Was back-and-through in perfect balance with an old time high finish. No wonder he won the Grand Slam — the British Open and Amateur as well as the U.S. Open and Amateur — all in the same year. You know the slam events have changed some over the years, but he's still the only man ever to win them all in one calendar year.

The third time I caddied for him, he arrived in Pinehurst early but wanted to enjoy Number 2 in the late afternoon. Guess he just liked the atmosphere...you know, when the sun begins to sit low in the sky and fills the clouds with the color of pink roses...gives a real peaceful feeling. Traffic on the course had cleared and we pretty much had the fairways to ourselves. I wanted to learn from the best so I memorized his every move in setting-up to the ball. Like all good golfers, his setup never varied.

"Willie, how long have you been caddying?" he asked me as he placed his ball on the first tee.

"Three years now, suh," I answered as I handed him his driver.

"You're not bad at reading greens for one so young," he noted, as he peered down the fairway from behind the ball.

"I hope so." Silently I prayed today wouldn't be the day I made a mistake.

He glanced at me. "Better be certain, son. When you give a golfer a read, tell him the truth or hold your tongue. If you hesitate, the golfer can't trust you. And that's a terrible thing."

His words came at me like a challenge and built-up my confidence. "Yes, suh, I know these greens."

He smiled. "Much better."

He set into the shot, planting his left heel opposite the ball and his right shoulder-width away from it. There was no keeping the feet together then separating them...no suh...not with Mr. Jones. He just set up like his feet knew exactly where they should go — natural as walking. I took note as he set his arms too. I followed the line of his left arm down through the shaft of the club. It changed direction just a touch, at his hands. The thumb and index finger appeared on his right hand as he cradled the left thumb in its palm. His grip of the club ran straight down — the perfect neutral grip. Kept wishing I had a camera the whole time I was studying him. He was like an instruction manual come to life. It was the ideal setup. He held it as I counted in my mind to three. This is the time when so many golfers get stiff through their body. But not Mr. Jones...he just relaxed like he was summoning all his flexibility to make that swing. On the way back his arms stayed on plane until his left shoulder settled under his chin. Fully coiled, he sorta tweaked his hands before dropping his arms into the slot. Was a different kinda move, but it worked real good for him. He unloaded until his right shoulder passed under his chin and pulled him to a high finish. That swing of his was a thing of true beauty...poetry even. To this day I never seen a better ball-striker than Bobby Jones. Well...maybe Byron Nelson, but no one else.

So here we were, just the two of us. I was walking the links of the greatest golf course in America with the greatest golfer in the world. I'd started out pretty nervous, but the longer we were out, the better I got at choosing clubs for Mr. Jones. So soon I wasn't

nervous at all and he started asking me the typical golf questions —
like — did I think I'd caddie long? Had I started playing yet? They
were questions I'd hear for years to come, but he asked me for a
different reason.

"I wish more of the boys down in Atlanta had the opportunity
you have here at Pinehurst," he said. "Too many kids there are
getting into trouble. Like they don't have enough to do."

"We get into trouble here, too," I confessed, "But my grandma
won't tolerate that from me none."

He smiled and rubbed the top of my head. "Good for her."

"Yeah, I've had the belt from her more than once."

"I'd like to meet this woman," he said, then winked. "Think she'd
like to come to Atlanta?"

I thought he was serious. "Oh, no," I said as strongly as I could,
and kinda panicked at the thought of my grandma taking off to go
live somewhere else. "She can't leave the farm."

He just chuckled and rubbed my head again. Bobby Jones and
me got along fine. I found myself opening up to him — probably
more than I shoulda, but he didn't seem to mind. I think he just got
a kick out of me. But then on the 14th green my comfort level
dropped like a rock.

"Well, Willie," he said. "What's this putt going to do?"

I lined up the 15-footer from behind the hole and walked careful
until I was behind the ball. From both angles it looked to bend more
than I knew it actually would. "Right to left break," I instructed.
"No more than a ball outside the hole."

"You sure about that?"

I remembered he didn't like my hesitancy the last time I answered his question about my knowledge of the greens. "Absolutely," I declared and silently prayed I was right.

I mighta answered bold this time, but I could sense he didn't quite trust my judgment. The golfer and the caddie are a team — have to be for the player to succeed. Was just like Mr. Jones said, it's a terrible thing when a golfer can't trust his caddie to make the right call. The player ends up losing confidence in his caddie and himself too.

Mr. Jones took more than his normal amount of time examining that putt. Not a good sign. Worse, when he set up to it, I could tell he was aimed too far right. Then he hit the ball too hard and through the break, leaving him a challenging four-footer coming back.

Told him I was sorry, but never in a million years did I expect the response he gave me.

"Don't be, Willie," he said. "You were right. I just hit a bad putt."

Now the rest of the round went real good, but all I could think about was that the man who might just be the greatest golfer of all time admitted to *me* that *he'd* made a mistake. Don't that beat all? For me his action defined his character, made him a man to admire for more than just his incredible playing ability. More than ever I wanted to learn all I could from him so I started asking him questions — probably too many questions. I wanted to know about golf...he wanted to tell me about life. Between those two subjects I left him that day a much richer boy.

To this day I hear his words each time I putt. "Don't pick up the putter going back because you'll lose control of the putt," he said.

"Straight back, low to the ground and straight through. Think about that, Willie."

I did. We were on the 17th green when he offered, "Here, take my putter."

He handed me the same club I'd drawn for him seventeen times that day, but when my hands touched it now, it was like I was holding something sacred from a church. He tossed a ball onto the green. "Take it back straight, low and slow." I did. "Now come through the same way." I did. "What did you learn?"

How to putt, I thought...but *what specifically?* "It helped me keep my head still," I replied.

"There you go."

As we came up the 18th, Mr. Jones said, "Willie, it's been quite a day. You've been good company, Son, and I hope we do this again soon."

Every time I caddied for that man...was a real treat for me. We'd talk about lotta things...so many can't rightly remember most of them now. But I do remember he brought the best out in me. I was always able talk to Bobby Jones. Never much mattered how different we were. He always talked to me like I was *somebody*. I got the feeling he was that way with most people. I just hoped they all appreciated him for that kindness like I did.

And I do recall the courses he told me he liked best.

"Number 2 of course. Love the angles into the greens," he told me that day we were alone. "Donald Ross brought a bit of the Old Course to America. Willie, don't you know that this is the St. Andrews of America?"

I knew St Andrews was where golf started. Back then that's *all* I knew.

"Is that right?" I answered.

"It surely is," he replied.

We walked a ways listening to the sounds a golf course makes. "You go to Florida a lot, too, huh?" I asked at length.

"Love Seminole in the south and Pine Valley up north," he said. "Forsgate's a good track up there as well."

"What about Pebble Beach?" I asked.

"Good course, but it's the ocean that makes it great," he said. "The Pacific can make any course great. But I prefer designs like Pinehurst where you take a piece of average land and carve it into magic."

So he rewarded Donald Ross' magic with some of his own. Mr. Jones especially liked holes 5, 9, 14, 16 and 18 — most probably 'cause he birdied them as many times as he parred them. Whenever I hear golf called the gentleman's game, I always think of Bobby Jones. Even though he was the best golfer of his time, Bobby Jones never turned pro 'cause professional golf in the '20s was frowned upon. Even in the '40s when the likes of Snead, Hogan, and Nelson came along, he resisted the temptation. Bobby Jones was locked into his law practice and that's where he'd stay. Three years after our last round together he was diagnosed with a rare spinal cord disease. Was such a shame...had to quit the game he loved all together. Sad thing, 1948 was the same year Donald Ross passed away. Losing both those special men was a massive blow to golf, but for me it was much more personal. I had looked up to them. They kinda defined golf for me back then and they ended up teaching me as much about life as about the game. Looking back on those simple rounds when I was barely a teenager, I know now how lucky I was. I didn't just carry their golf bags, I got to talk to them, laugh with them...really *know* them as men. So maybe I'm bragging but I like to believe they were just meant to be there for me in my early years.

Bobby Jones finally surrendered to his crippling disease in 1971. Three years later he rightly was inducted into the World Golf Hall of Fame in its inaugural year...and back then, of course, the Hall was in Pinehurst.

Walter Hagan enjoys a smoke as he blasts from the bunker during the 1933 North South Open.

CHAPTER FOUR

THE HAIG
AND THE SQUIRE

*T*hat room gets so quiet after I tell my story about Bobby Jones, all you could hear is ice clinking in their glasses. I scan the faces. I can see them trying to sort out their own thoughts about that great golfer. As for me...I'm still taken by just how personal the passing of Mr. Jones and Mr. Ross was for me and how lucky I was to know them both. Only 'cause of people like those two I'm standing here tonight...the center of attention.

"Caddying for the Great Bobby Jones," says red tie. "Now that must have been an honor."

I nod, still remembering. "Yes, suh, and way more than that."

"Francis Oiumet, now he has to have been before your time, Willie," someone cracks from far back in the crowd.

"Sure was," I reply. "But I know he won the North South one year."

"There were a bunch of good players back then," the paisley tie remarks. "I just can't think of them now."

"Two stand out in my mind," adds green tie, "Gene Sarazen and the irascible Walter Hagen. Did you ever caddie for either of them?"

Their names trigger more memories and stories. "Both," I tell him.

Walter Hagen

Pure and simple, Mr. Hagen, fondly dubbed "Sir Walter, The Haig," was a character.

"Everybody's a celebrity regardless of what they do," he announced shortly after I met him. I drew him for one of the North South tournaments in the '40s. He was *fun* to be around...laughed a lot...always acted like life was his personal stage, made just so he could show off his talent. He approached life all carefree and did the same with golf. Now he wasn't the straightest striker of the ball but it didn't matter 'cause trouble on the course didn't seem to faze him none. Fact is, I think he kinda enjoyed problem shots 'cause they gave him one more chance to entertain the galleries. Fairway golf woulda bored the man. He enjoyed the risks...taking chances. "Shots you never get to practice," he told me. "Those are the ones that keep this game interesting."

To this day I'm not sure how much his routine was act and how much was real. But I can tell you that buried beneath the happy-go-lucky front he put out to the public was a *fierce* competitor. More than most players, I think, Walter Hagen leaned on a friendly bottle to help get him through a round...so maybe he was a little worried, too.

"Willie," he told me as we walked down the 1st hole of Number 2, "You might find my bag a tad heavier than others you tote."

"Suh?"

He measured me...young teenager that I was. Then I caught his anxious look. He'd seen me glance wide-eyed at the bottle cap peeking out of the pocket of his golf bag...of course he had no way of knowing my dad was a drinking man too. "You see, I carry a substance in my bag that helps me make some mighty outrageous shots from time-to-time." He said it real casual and all matter-of-fact like but was quick to add, "Of course, it's legal."

I cocked my head. "Yes suh. My dad likes vodka."

He broke into a warm smile and said, "Then we understand each other. I'm glad to see that. Now I'll tell you when I need it," he said. "And when I do, just set the bag down and look the other way. I'll do the rest."

The first time he needed a boost came on at the 2nd hole and I remember wondering right then if he'd driven his ball into the pine trees on the right on purpose, just for an opportunity to steal a swig. We found his ball. He stood there looking at it, considering the lie offering not much more than its skinny opening through the trees. That's when he announced, "Willie, it's time to set the bag down."

Well, I done what he asked and he pulled out a fifth of *Johnnie Walker Red*, drank from the bottle, capped it and squeezed it back into the bag. Then he didn't hesitate a minute. He drew his 5-iron from the bag, set the ball well back in his stance, and struck a low-liner that just missed a menacing maze of pines by maybe a hair. His ball fled those trees like a bird set loose. It landed in front of the green and rolled some to about 15 feet of the hole.

"Bottled magic...you've got to love it," he proclaimed to me with a smile. You could hear the crowd's amazement in response to his spectacular shot. "Let's go."

Walter Hagen didn't win the tournament that year, but it was a pleasure to share the course with him. We talked about caddying and especially about Number 2. He told me Donald Ross' creation was one of the best courses in the world. "The angles to these greens and the small landing areas on them are things of beauty, my lad," he said. It was no accident that he was such an accomplished golfer...under all his bluster was a serious and knowledgeable student of the game. But his showman side with its lighthearted attitude kept everyone loose...caddies loved working with him...players enjoyed his company. He was a touring pro when the best amateurs of the day refused to turn pro. Most likely they were scared, being the notion of professional golfers was frowned upon back then. I expect public opinion managed to back off a bunch of them who mighta turned pro otherwise. Although he never told me so, I think this discrimination bothered him some, so he purposely used his antics to annoy the elite.

Don't get me wrong...Walter Hagen was a first-class player 'cause of his first-class swing. Now looking at him...he didn't fit the stature of most golfers...so you wouldn't think he'd have the smooth swing he did...*and he could repeat it, too!* To the casual observer, he swung that club with no effort...no effort at all. But to a caddie's analyzing eye, every tiny detail of his swing was perfectly timed and always the same...might even be tempted to call it mechanical...it was *that* constant. But then someone would think I meant Walter Hagan had stiffness in his swing...and that he never did.

The last time I caddied for him he had five birdies for a 67 on Number 2, and that included one on his favorite holes, the relatively short 3rd.

Gene Sarazen

I'm sure most people know about Gene Sarazen's double eagle in the 1935 Masters, but what I bet most people *don't* know is, that more than any of his golfing achievements, Mr. Sarazen believed his greatest accomplishment and contribution to the game was him inventing the sand wedge. God's truth...a short man, Gene Sarazen proved size don't matter in golf. Anyone who played him best be prepared to *run* around the course, 'cause to this day, he was one of the fastest players I ever caddied for. So it wasn't surprising that in the autumn of his golfing career, he teamed up regular with another quickie, Julius Boros.

I got to caddie for Mr. Sarazen several times, all of them long before he'd been nicknamed "The Squire" on account of him buying a farm for his family up in New York State. But the match I remember best was in 1948 when Mr. Boros and him took on Art Wall and Denny Shute.

I think that best-ball match probably was over before it even started. Right on the first tee, Mr. Sarazen laid down a defining marker, "Gentlemen, you see the pathway running from the tee to the fairway," he said referring to the short green carpet flanked on both sides by heavy rough. "We all know what that is. *Hogan's Pathway.* And we all know what it's for, I reckon. If you hit your drive in the fairway, you can walk to your ball by way of the pathway. If not, you walk off in the rough...any questions?"

Mr. Sarazen gave a perfect description of *Hogan's Pathway.* Ben Hogan didn't like getting his shoes dirty or wet...didn't think golfers who hit good drives should have to ruin their shoes. So, he created

Gene Sarazan (L) and Sam Snead (R)
enjoy a light moment on the driving range, "Maniac Hill."

the pathway that runs tee to fairway on any respectable golf course. That day Denny Shute and Art Wall missed about four or five fairways apiece while my twosome had just one wrong drive between them. Now their rivals never complained so as anyone could hear, but us caddies knew that walking the rough bothered them...well, that and the pace of play, of course. This match was all about gamesmanship and Gene Sarazen had stacked the deck.

He told me our first time out, "When you give me a club, I'm ready to go." *Man he wasn't kidding!* I know *I* was pretty much winded when we finished Number 2 in less than two and a half hours.

My team won the 1st hole and needed the 2nd to start the press. As usual, Sarazen and Boros were neck-and-neck down the middle of the fairway with their tee shots. Both men hit their drives about the same distance, but I knew that Mr. Boros hit his irons a bit longer. Without hesitating I handed Mr. Sarazen a 4-iron. He hit confidently and planted the ball five plus feet from the hole. But when I drew a 5-iron for Mr. Boros, he stopped me.

"No offense, but you gave Sarazen a 4-iron."

"I did, suh," I said. "But I believe you hit your irons a tad longer than Mr. Sarazen."

My answer raised Mr. Boros' eyebrows, but when he glanced at his partner, Gene Sarazen shrugged and never said a word. "Let's go with the 5 then," Boros said. He took the club, made the shot and started walking even before the ball landed to rest one foot from the hole. *What a fabulous stroke!* Julius Boros had what I like to call a sugary swing — simple and sweet. He didn't take the club back

Julius Boros warming up for the 1948 North South Open

as far as most golfers of his time, but he sure could hit it as far as almost anyone. His distance amazed me 'cause he wasn't a big man and he never showed much effort in his swing.

After they won the 2nd hole, *nobody* was questioning my club choice. The foursome halved the 3rd hole, but my team won 5 and 6 and kept the press on. After halving 7 and 8, we reached the halfway house. Mr. Sarazen, always treated the caddies and his partners to food and drink, but this time he threw in some gamesmanship for good measure.

"You're both bleeding rather profusely at this point," he smiled to Wall and Shute. "I'll get the refreshments all around. Keep your money for later. You'll need it."

Sure enough, we won the 9th hole.

Fact my team never lost a hole that day. We won with a birdie on 10, halved 11 and 12, won 13 with a birdie, halved 14 and 15, won 16 and halved 17.

"You guys are in tough shape," Mr. Boros told them as they stood on the 18th tee.

"You *did* bring your wallets, didn't you," his partner added with a cat-that-swallowed-the-canary smile.

The jabbing was in good fun and their rivals took it like gentlemen.

"Tell you what," Mr. Sarazen went on. "Do you want to press us on the last? Say double or nothing for the whole match."

"You're on," snapped Mr. Wall.

The opposing team put up a good fight, but the best they could do was halve the hole.

"Next time *we'll* take Willie," Denny Shute groused as they came off the green.

"Not on your life," Mr. Sarazen cracked. "He's *my* caddie. Julius and I will take on anyone with McRae on our bags. Right, Willie?"

I raised my brows but kept quiet. Now I greatly appreciated that compliment, but those two coulda handled the best on any given day with or without the likes of me. In a best-ball on Number 2, they shot a real regular five or six under...when players can do that, it's a treat just being part of the action.

The 1951 U.S. Ryder Cup Team

CHAPTER FIVE

THE 1951 RYDER CUP

*B*y now that group of suits and ties around me has got about three deep. "After that round," I tell them, "I knew I wanted to caddie for all the important people... all the people who'd left their mark...and I've caddied for my share of them."

I hear my "audience" chuckle...a few of them nod.

"Rumor has it you once caddied for Charles Barkley," asks a man two deep from me. "Is his swing as bad as it looks on TV?"

I shake my head and say, "There just ain't no way to help that man. Now Yogi Berra...he didn't look like much in knickers, but that man was sneaky good."

"He must have been quite the character," comments a man with a drink in his hand.

"Sure was," I tell him. "He was a regular at Pinehurst during the '60s and '70s...used to bring his family and friends along and liked driving his grandkids around the place. Once he brought just about half the Yankee team...played that weekend for big stakes, too."

"Who came?" another man I can hardly see pipes up from the back.

*Yogi Berra on golf – "Eighty percent of the balls
that don't reach the hole, don't go in."*

"Who didn't," I reply. "Mantle and Ford, Hank Bauer, Moose Skowron, bunch of others. Anyway...that Sunday Yogi, and some fella whose name just won't come to me, played Mickey and Whitey. What a circus..."

"How so?" cuts in someone.

"For the life of me don't know why they did it," I say, "But they let Yogi play from the red tees. Did he snooker them but good. See, he was grousing so much about being short off the tee compared to those muscle men that by Sunday, they let him play from the reds. And no matter how hard they tried, Mantle and Ford just couldn't take a hole."

A chorus of, "No kidding" fills the room.

"When all seemed lost, the two would try to put Yogi down, but he tossed them his classic one-liners like a tennis star volleying with amateurs.

"Like what?" someone calls.

"Mantle would crack, 'Didn't think women were allowed out here today.' Yogi would let it pass like water down a duck's back. 'I'm a catcher and can catch anything you can throw at me. I'll put a dress on too, but I'm hitting from the reds.' He got them but good, especially on the 16th, par 5. The match was done and Yogi, like he had a bunch of times earlier, outdrove his buddies. As he walked on ahead of them, he glanced over his shoulder and called, 'You wanna go through?' I shake my head. 'Ol' Yogi...now he was a good one."

While I'm still thinking back on that weekend, someone barks, "What about Michael Jordan? I remember he was thinking about *going pro at one time. Was he that good?"*

"Only in his mind," I answer truly hoping that would be the end of it.

But no, that man just had to keep on. "You caddied for him then?"

"I did," I tell him. "Don't get me wrong. He hit the ball pretty big."

"Did he bring Number 2 to its knees?"

"Not exactly...more like in the 80s."

"Really!" another exclaims. "I thought he was better than that."

"So did he. But he was a good guy. Called me Pop."

"So who was the best pro athlete you ever caddied for?"

Have to think about this one. "Been some great ones out there...Jerry Rice...what a fine athlete. He shot a 74 from the tips and man could he clobber the ball!"

"What was he like?"

"Super guy," I say. "Told him he owed me a lot of money I lost betting against him, but that he could keep it all if he'd just teach me how to dance. He won that TV show, you know, the one called 'Dancing with the Stars.' "

"So, he was the best?"

I shake my head. "Didn't say that. Julius Erving...now he could play with the golfing greats and give them a run for their money."

"Then Dr. J —"

"Didn't say that neither." I wink. "But he comes close."

"Then who was it?"

"Peyton Manning shot a 70 from the tips," I say.

"Peyton Manning, wow," someone comments from the back. "I didn't know he played golf."

"Oh. Then there was Lawrence Taylor," I add.

"One of the greatest linebackers of all time," someone notes. "He was the best?"

"Well, he shot 70 from the tips of 2 with four three-putts."

Heads shake and jaws go slack in disbelief.

"What was the best round of golf you ever saw?" another asks. The transition is so sudden it kinda jolts me a bit. Have to stop and think. But then all them memories flood my mind and I feel a smile crease my face. Now I caddied for the best over the years, so there's lot of good golf rounds to remember. But to this day I remember right near every shot of that one special round played more than half a century ago.

"It ended in a tie," I tell them.

Dad was a drinker, bless his soul. By 1944 his problem caught up with him real bad like. Edna Taylor, long time teacher at the Taylortown School, well she was one of those rare teachers who really cared about her students. So one day when she saw Dad passed out under our *Tree of Knowledge,* she just went on over and splashed a bucket of water right in his face. He woke sudden but drunk-dazed, and she told him right then and there he was going in the army, no ands, ifs, buts, about it. She drafted him herself...and just like that he was gone. Dad served overseas a few years. Then one day he drove a jeep over a German mine. Well, it plum tore out the insides of the vehicle and left Dad in rough shape...had so many injuries he got sent home.

Happened in 1946. By then I was just about 15. While Dad was away, lessons from Grandma and chats with Mollie Mae had kept me out of trouble. They taught me to keep my complaints and sass to myself, so I managed to become an established caddie. Then too people like Fletcher, George Dunlap and Tommy Curry, all had helped me find my way around a golf course. They showed patience 'cause of my age and I thank God I was smart enough to take their lessons to heart. After a while I started finding my reward in "A" evaluations. See after each round, golfers are asked to rate their caddies "A" through "D." Most of the evaluations were about technical skill, reading the greens, clubbing the player...but "A" caddies had to excel in one more important area – *attitude.*

Richard Tufts once told me, "I like the way you carry yourself, Willie."

That was the day I caddied for both Mr. Ross and Mr. Tufts. When we came to the 3rd hole, Mr. Tufts hit his drive – just like always – right down the middle of the fairway, but this time, it was just a little fat. He was between clubs for his approach shot.

"What do you think, Willie?"

Usually Mr. Tufts was a smooth mashie away. "The 8," I said with conviction.

The golfer grimaced. "Not sure about this," he remarked as he shook his head. "But if you say so, Willie, the 8 it is."

He lined up the shot much longer than normal. Once he settled into his stance, he shuffled his feet. He just couldn't get set. I knew he was trying to convince himself I was right but all he was doing was making an easy shot a lot harder than it had to be.

"Just hit it, suh," I urged.

He gave me a short nod and struck the ball. But when it took flight, I thought the shot was too long...started thinking just about then this was gonna be one long painful round of golf. But the ball fooled me — it was dead on the stick. Now if it could be the right distance too...Unbelievably...it *was*. Darn if it didn't hit just three feet past the pin and roll back into the hole so fast you'd think rain was coming and it was looking for cover.

Now Mr. Ross complimented Mr. Tufts on his play that day, but I could tell his competitive spirit got kinda dampened. So fortunately just one week later, on that very same hole, I handed that accomplished golf architect a 9-iron and he ended up matching his friend's success. Nice how things work out sometimes...

Moments like that boosted my evaluations even more.

So my reputation already was pretty solid when Mr. Tufts showed up to play with his son in tow. Peter was just one year older than me, and still struggling to find his game. We played about the same so he was real easy to club right from the start. The tips I gave him on the greens were spot on so after just nine holes we were chatting like brothers. After 18 holes he slapped me on the shoulder. "Well done. I like your style."

From then on we were real good friends. At first I only caddied for Peter, but before long he invited me to golf with him.

"This is ridiculous," Peter said when he looked at my sad collection of three or four clubs. "If you're going to play with me, Willie, you need a real set of clubs. I'll talk to my dad...he can take care of that."

I guess with Peter being part of Pinehurst's royal family, he could just flat out say something like that, like it was a done deal. Sure enough, in 1950 his father gave me my first full set of golf clubs. To this day, I'm still in awe, about how a poor African American growing up in the South rubbed elbows so easy with people like the Tufts. But I figure it came down to two things: *mutual acceptance and respect.* From the time I was just a school kid, Richard Tufts always treated me like a grown man. And Peter...well nothing ever seemed to bother him much. He was comfortable with me like he was with his well-to-do classmates...maybe even more so. Mr. Tufts and his son both showed me respect and treated me like family. That's just the way the Tufts were. They wanted everyone – dignitaries visiting Pinehurst and employees alike – not just to *feel* like family, but to *be* family. They knew the key to family is showing each other respect...and I firmly believe that's true.

One day when I was playing with Peter, he just didn't seem like himself. Was edgy...almost irritable...we played the first several holes in awkward silence. I knew something was bothering him but had a feeling I shouldn't be asking about it.

After he managed to push his approach shot into the pine straw on the 8th hole of Number 2, he finally spit it out. "Willie," he said, "We have a problem here at the resort."

"Yeah," I said. "What's that?"

"It's about some of the caddies." He measured me to see how I took the comment.

I shrugged. "Oh?"

"They're not all like you, Willie," he continued. "Attitude-wise...you know what I mean...Dad's noticed it...Mr. Ross, too."

"You talking about some of the younger ones?"

"A few — but some older than you, too."

Not sure where this conversation was headed, I volunteered, "Think I can help?"

Peter smiled with obvious relief. "Hoped you'd say that," he admitted.

From then on, if a caddie sassed a member or guest, forgot to wipe off clubs, or just plain forgot his place on the course, I'd sit down with him and try to set him straight. We'd go into the caddie room and have a one-on-one. Of course it didn't always go so good. Sometimes a caddie would get all huffy 'cause he felt like he was being grilled by a peer. Then there were others who flat out resented me for having a special relationship with the Tufts...thought I was privileged. For the most part, though, the tactic worked good enough. After I'd have a sit-down heart-to-heart, Peter would come into the room. Always got kinda nervous when he came in 'cause I wasn't sure how the caddie would react. But mostly the caddie ended up promising to "work on things."

My training efforts didn't hurt my evaluations neither. A little before Donald Ross passed away in 1948, Mr. Tufts took me aside and thanked me for my help. "I'm going to get you a bag for the '51 Ryder Cup," he promised. I like to think my "A" evaluation woulda earned me a bag without his endorsement. But with the main man in my corner, I was a shoe-in. Didn't matter I was the youngest "A" caddie by about 10 years 'cause *only* "A" performers got a bag for the event.

ON THE BAG

That year the players from the United States and Great Britain were all supposed to arrive for practice rounds on Thursday. So, the night before twenty-four of us gathered in the caddie room to draw straws to see whose bag we'd be toting. Strong favor was on our American side 'cause we had a real impressive field. Ben Hogan stood down as captain to let Sam Snead step in. Oh they *all* were there...the sharp-dresser, Jimmy Demaret...Horton Smith...Jackie Burke...all of them. I closed my eyes, reached into the hat and hoped to snag one of the Americans. When we'd all drawn, we opened our folded pieces of paper real slow with anticipation. I was just holding my breath...knew I had a fifty-fifty chance of getting an American and one in 24 of getting Ben Hogan. But it wasn't meant to be...I ended up with Fred Daly, the mainstay on the British team.

On the first day of the tournament, the temperature barely hit thirty-two degrees. I met Mr. Daly just as he came out of the clubhouse. Right away I felt guilty for being disappointed at drawing the Brit. Fred Daly was a class act. As things turned out...he'd make my Ryder Cup not just fun...but *real* educational.

Like everyone else we headed for the driving range. Back then the Pinehurst range was real narrow. The players stood at one end while us caddies took our places in the field. We called it the *hot zone* 'cause they shot everything at us except the kitchen sink. We had to keep track of our player's shots — then gather up all the balls fast as we could. They shot everything from drivers to 9-irons at us. The less accurate shots, of course, often found a competitor's caddie as target. I wince every time I remember how I caught *four* stray shots that first day. We were told to absorb the pain best we could and move on. "A" caddies, well...it's just what we did...what we were expected to do as part of the job...and for the most part we really didn't care about getting hit. *This was the Ryder Cup.*

The Ryder Cup in 1951 featured two 36-hole events. There were four Best-Ball foursomes on Friday and eight single matches on Sunday. *So what do you think did they did on Saturday?* Traveled to Raleigh to watch the University of North Carolina football game, can you beat that? Friday was raw — temperature barely scraped above freezing. The wind, brutal from the west, didn't help. But this was the biggest day of my life so I had to block it out. Kept hearing dad's words — *"Show up, shut up 'n keep up"* — ringing in my ears. Forget the cold — just get it done right.

Fortunately I was in the clean-up foursome. It featured Ben Hogan and Jimmy Demaret for the United States and Fred Daly with Ken Bousfield for Great Britain. Players and fans both milled around as each foursome teed off. When the foursome left the tee, I noticed everyone was chatting, everyone that is except Ben Hogan...he was busy putting on his camel hair overcoat.

His caddie, Fletcher Gaines, leaned toward me and muttered, "He's too small to be good as they say...and with that overcoat his swing won't hold up, you'll see."

"I don't get it," I replied between my chattering teeth. "Not only is he itty bitty, but he damn near died in that car accident a couple of years ago. How they think he's gonna be able to get the job done?"

"I think this cold's gonna wear him out quick," said Joe Tyson, Demaret's caddie. "Don't know why any of us wanted to get on *his* bag. If I was a betting man, I'd put my two cents on the Brits today."

Joe woulda lost that bet...and lost *big*.

After being announced on the first tee, Hogan looked at the other players, then at us and said, "Have a good round." Besides making brief and sparse conversation with Demaret, Ben Hogan didn't utter another word until the match was over. His size didn't matter neither, and his overcoat never did slow him down. Every shot he made bowed real slight like to the right, no more than four inches I'd say. Using an interlocking grip, the back of his right hand pointed square down the shaft. No matter which club he used, he planted that perfect neutral grip on the shaft just like he'd invented it himself. Since Hogan never spoke, Fletcher would just draw a club and hand it to the man...was always the right club too. Hogan never questioned a selection. Fletcher Gaines was *that* good. Had to be...*it was the Ryder Cup...and this was Ben Hogan.*

"My man's doing *great*, y'all," he bragged as we walked.

"Not what you thought on the 1st tee," Tyson remarked.

"That was *then*," Gaines replied. "Hogan's *smoking*."

The man was so good the match almost got boring. While us caddies struggled to keep warm, Hogan seemed to birdie everything in sight...and it didn't seem to matter if he wasn't dead on the pin with his approach shots. He could get up and down from almost anywhere.

When we came to the long 11th hole, Fletcher whispered, "Bet he birdies this one, too."

Tyson cracked, "He always birdies this hole. How many times he played here?"

"A bunch," I answered.

"And he's never had more than a three on this hole."

"Does that mean you concede the hole?" Fletcher said looking real smug. He raised his eyebrows. *"Think on it now...it's 32 degrees and he's got that overcoat flapping below his knees. What do you say?"*

We were smart not to take the bet. Hogan did birdie the hole. This "itty-bitty" man was so much larger than life that frigid morning. He brought the fabled 7,007-yard Pinehurst Number 2 to its knees, finishing the round on his ball alone, 32 − 34 for a 66. When you think about all of it...the weather, the bulky clothing − not to mention hitting and *never* questioning a club handed to him − it was easy to see how this golfer won the '51 Masters and '50 U.S. Open. How anyone could survive the horrible car accident he did and go on to accomplish what he did is remarkable...truly remarkable. It was a pleasure and an honor to caddie in that morning's foursome. Over lunch between rounds, we were so busy reliving nearly every stroke that we hardly found time to eat. But Hogan never showed emotion. Just took each shot in turn...and when all eight of us came off the 18th green around noon, Mr. Hogan wished everybody a good day...just like he'd done on the 1st tee. Those were the only words I heard him utter in all 18 holes.

The afternoon round was all over but the shout. Oh, the Brits made a comeback of sorts, but it was almost like Mr. Hogan was playing cat-and-mouse with them. Just when their hopes started rising, he slammed the door shut by draining a few critical putts to close them out 5 and 4.

Was that morning round *the best* I ever saw? Maybe...sure thought so after that round was over...couldn't stop raving about that itty-bitty fellow at home that night. But two days later, I think my man's afternoon round, Fred Daly's round, was even better. Daly drew Clayton Heafner in the singles pairings and lost the morning round by three strokes, 70 to 73. Lunch musta been painful for him. The Brits were getting beat at every turn and the bitter cold wasn't helping them a bit. By mid-afternoon, the outcome of the 1951 Ryder was known — another American victory. One-by-one the matches closed with lopsided U.S. wins. Losing the morning round and beginning the afternoon session in the deepest of holes, it woulda been easy for Mr. Daly to fold too. How could anyone summon the courage to fight on at that point?

Now like I said before, there's a trust that builds up between a player and his caddie...has to be if the golfer is gonna score his best in a pressure cooker like the Ryder Cup. For me at age 18, just having a man like Fred Daly tip his cap in my direction was reward enough...but to have almost constant conversation for 36 holes with such a man — *incredible*...just an incredible experience. Even though I was an American and he was a Brit, we were bonding for a common purpose. He couldn't turn to anyone else but me and I couldn't turn to anyone else but him. Nothing mattered but our mission...not color, not where we came from, not how much money we had — or didn't. It was all about winning the match.

"What do you think, Willie?" he asked me on the 5th hole.

Now mostly he was a cheerful man, but I remember thinking he sounded kinda down just then. For good reason, too...I think the cold was finally wearing him out. I sensed he was considering an early out, maybe ending the agony on the 11th or 12th hole. It would be embarrassing, but the whole tournament already was that way for the Brits.

"You're only four down," I replied. "And we got plenty of holes left."

He looked at me. I could tell he was weighing the simple arithmetic of what I said. "You're right," he said with a wry smile. But he didn't sound too convincing. "Let's see what we can do about that."

Soon after that point, the death call for the Brits grew louder. We couldn't hardly hear the polite applause for our friends from across the "pond" over the unmistakable cheers for the Americans. Like all the caddies, I wanted the Americans to win, but I felt embarrassed for my golfer. I liked him. Found myself wanting him to succeed even though he *was* a Brit. Right about then nothing woulda made me happier than for Mr. Daly to crush the likeable Mr. Heafner.

My man took the 13th hole to pull back within three strokes. I made a fist and told him, "We're gonna *win*."

His lips creased into that wry little smile again. I handed him his driver for the 14th. He said nothing.

"No really," I insisted. "The wheels are gonna come off Mr. Heafner."

He played real good but tied Mr. Heafner on the next two holes. He came to the 16th tee dormie — three down with three to play.

"A tie's better than a loss," I encouraged, *"All you gotta to do is win the next three holes."*

"I like your enthusiasm, Willie," he replied, "but I'd have to at least birdie every one left."

"If that's what it takes, suh, *do it*," I said.

Don't know if it was my tone or the words themselves that startled Mr. Daly. Only when he straightened did I realize how demanding I musta sounded.

Both men ripped their tee shots right down the middle. But this was a good sign. Now Mr. Daly didn't outdrive his opponent very often...but he did on this challenging par 5...and the Brit stayed ahead of his rival on the next shot, too. Mr. Heafner pulled his second shot left, close to a bunker while my player striped it dead straight again. I don't know if it was the cold or the length of the round, but now I saw a crack in the American's armor. On his simple 9-iron approach, Mr. Heafner yanked the ball left of the flag.

"I told you Mr. Heafner's wheels would be coming off," I said. I handed Mr. Daly a 9-iron and caught new optimism in his eye. "Hit it three quarters."

And he *did* — spot on the pin. The ball landed three feet past the stick and we watched it curl up about a foot from the hole. Down two with two to go.

On the 17th tee, I flung a bit of grass in the air. The wind was straight in our faces now and if anything the temperature had dropped a degree or two since morning. I reached for the 4-iron, but Mr. Daly grabbed my arm and winked. "The 5," he said.

He surprised me and I wasn't too sure about that 5-iron but I handed him his club of choice. Now maybe it was 'cause there was nothing left to lose or maybe it was all that adrenaline pumping through his veins, but he smoothed that 5-iron. The ball hit near the pin, hopped once and stuck like it knew where to go all along — one foot from the hole. I'd underestimated the turning point on 16. Fred Daly was pumped. Now I saw confidence in the twinkle of those eyes...confidence I hadn't seen in our first 70 holes. He strutted away from the tee markers like a man refreshed. Golf is a mental game...truly is...and by the time you reach this point in a match, most things can get to look pretty negative. Mr. Daly sensed that's what was happening with his rival and it only made him stronger. He was striking the ball straight and long. Each shot energized his spirits more. He was in the *zone*. From here on out he would choose his clubs and nail the shots. Since we were a team, his confidence rubbed off on me. I didn't care that we were playing for the pride of England; I was more interested in helping the lone Brit survivor get it done.

Clayton Heafner hit a brilliant tee shot, but that nagging hook kept the ball a testy eight feet from the hole. He conceded Mr. Daly's putt but then took about twice the normal time lining up his own. I think he realized his wheels weren't so steady no more...that maybe draining this putt was his best, maybe the last chance to win. Momentum swings are true tests of courage. That day I discovered just how real they were.

From the moment the club head hit the ball, I knew that ball was in the cup. Like a dart the ball scampered toward the hole dead on. But suddenly it was like the Queen of England herself swooped down and ordered what happened next. That ball ground to a halt no more than a hair width from the lip of the cup. We all watched for the better part of a minute, but it stubbornly refused to drop.

One down with one to go.

On the 18th, both men drilled their drives down the left side of the fairway. I figured Mr. Daly was on a roll and didn't really need me except to haul his clubs. After testing the wind though, he scowled.

"The 6," I said, surprised that he hadn't reached the same conclusion. "Smooth a 6."

Never hesitated, just took the club, set up and did just like I instructed. We both watched the ball pierce through the fierce wind and land safe in the middle of the green. We could see the pressure build on Clayton Heafner. Tie or win didn't matter so much in the greater scheme of things. The United States had already won the 1951 Ryder Cup. The final score was 9.5 to 2.5. But this late afternoon rivalry had become something else — that personal thing where two competitors had to reach down deep to overcome. *Who was the better man?*

That day it was Fred Daly. Mr. Heafner hit his second shot a tad fat. That crippling hook landed his approach in the bunker left of the green. As he planted his feet, I could tell he sensed defeat. He just about made the apron on his sand blast. He putted onto the green, but didn't need to finish. Mr. Daly ran his putt to within a foot and a half and the match was over, all square.

For 36 holes two great golfers fought to a draw. Yet for one it was victory, the other defeat. I had the opportunity to caddie several times after that for Clayton Heafner. I like to think he wanted me on his bag either to bring him good luck or to keep away bad.

There were many great rounds played in those two days of the 1951 Ryder Cup. Everything about Hogan's round had been unforgettable – the cold, the dress, the way he carried himself. Then there was John Alexander. Less than a year earlier that poor man had been burned on over seventy percent of his body in a bad car wreck, yet he won his 36-hole match over John Panton 8 and 7, and did it with his hands bleeding for most of the match. But Fred Daly gave me something *special* in those last 18 holes. He showed me a man can succeed when it looks most like he can't. It takes a special quality...something rare...something you can't wrap your arms around. Some people have it and others don't. The ones who don't probably don't even know something like that exists. But knowing it exists and seeing it firsthand on that mean cold day made me want to be a caddie even more...and not just be *any* caddie, but the *best* caddie. And I learned something else too. Before that day I'd enjoyed my experiences...liked a lot of the players I'd looped for, too. But in that round I learned how critical it was for golfer and caddie to be a *solid team* in a competitive event. Don't think there's a better way to learn about another man...and I know for certain, there's no way more special.

As I walked home that night, there was new energy in my step. From that day on I wanted to rub elbows with as many famous people as I could. Wanted to find out what makes them tick and see what I could learn from them.

Pinehurst gave me the stage to do just that. It took some time for me to add to the learning of that day. Over the years I've come to understand that important people are no more special than ordinary folks. Great people exist at every level and every level has its share of jerks. But if you treat everybody the way you want them treating you, and they treat you that way back, you'll get the most out of each other...see everyone for who he really is, too. Golf's got its own way of making all that real clear and no one sees it better than a well-trained caddie.

*View of the Pinehurst Clubhouse from the left rough
of the 18th hole of Number 2.*

CHAPTER SIX

THE MONEY ROUND

I finish telling about the 1951 Ryder Cup and glance around at all them suits surrounding me. I bet they're thinking the best game I ever saw was that great frosty morning round of Ben Hogan's. Technically...probably was...But I think I learned more from Fred Daly in his singles match. What I learned from that match has helped me through all these years in so many other matches...and I'm not talking just about the ones I caddied for...no suh, what I learned from that match helped me with my own game, too.

"Now it wasn't a complete bust for the Brits," I say.

"How's that?" asks the man to my left, ready for another story.

"Well, for one thing, Arthur Lacey, the Brits' team captain, he ended up staying."

My knowing smile causes confused frowns. "Why?" someone ventures.

"Because would you believe he came to meet his future wife on the golf course that week?"

Raised brows now melt into a mix of subtle chuckles, sniffs and snorts.

"Her name was Mildred," I tell them. "She was a fine woman — had her own money, too — a genuine woman of means. Miss Mildred supported the kindergarten in Taylortown and did her share to fix up that building. She was something...came to read to the kids real regular. My sister, Costella, worked for her."

"How did she and Lacey meet?" another asks.

"Miss Mildred owned a house next to the 5th tee on Number 2," I reply. "I seem to recall she told my sister she walked all 72 holes those two days. Now some say Miss Mildred was looking for a husband when she was doing all that walking, but I don't know that's true. Never heard that's what she said. I think she just met Mr. Lacey when he was watching his players practice on the range. Anyway they met at some point and before it was all over, I'm sure she did her best to console the poor captain."

"Did they get married right after the Cup?" someone asks.

"No" I answer. "He courted her for nearly two weeks before they tied the knot. But he never went back to England. Later on they had a pretty bad car wreck but were lucky...they came through it okay...guess you could say they lived happily ever after."

The suits fall quiet, drinking in what's probably the best story about the 1951 Ryder Cup. Nice to know two people coming from such different backgrounds could connect with such a special love. Now I don't know about others, but I always felt real good about that couple.

"Did you get nervous during the Ryder Cup matches?" asks another suit.

I think a moment, but it doesn't take long to come up with an answer. "Not near as nervous as I got during the money matches!"

In 1949 Dad took to drinking unbelievable heavy. Was bad...real bad...but he still caddied and worked at Carolina Pharmacy. Well, he'd survived having twelve kids and driving an army Jeep over a German mine, so I guess he felt entitled to down a few. His friends used to come over and they'd all set around under our *Tree of Knowledge* and drink until they couldn't drink no more. I do believe their carrying on contributed to my coming-of-age. I was driving by then so it was up to me to get them all home. Dad would tell me when it was time to collect the bodies and then I'd gather them all up and drive them home. The ones controlled enough would slap me on the back when they could manage. Sometimes I'd even get a slurred "thank you" thrown my way.

But I remember one night after the Ryder Cup it was just dad and me under that tree.

He offered me a drink. I thought was just 'cause he was in a drinking mood and I was the only one around. But looking back I think he asked me 'cause that was the first time he saw me as a man. He poured us each a drink. But when I saw the expression that came to his eyes after I asked that first question, I knew this wasn't going be no long drinking night. No suh...I figured we'd both still be sober — or close to it — when it ended.

"Why did you name our tree the *Tree of Knowledge?*"

Our eyes met and just then I saw clear...probably for the first time...how his were filled with the quiet collected wisdom of an adult.

I realized at that moment I still had a long way to go to get to where that man was. " 'Cause this is a place where you can set around and learn from others, son," he said. "Melvin and Kurt and the others, we all got a *lot* of time behind us...we get together here, yeah...to bullshit some...but mostly to reflect...measure where we been, mistakes we made, weigh what we done...stuff like that."

"So drinking makes it weigh less?" I smirked like the wise-ass kid I still could be.

"You know what I mean," he growled, was thoughtful for a moment, then added, "We done all right...got married, raised kids, provided for our families...for the most part, anyway."

"Yes, you did," I agreed.

He studied me. I knew he was trying to tell if I really meant it. I did. "Son, we been blessed here in the Pinehurst area," he said.

"What do you mean?"

He sniffed. I had no idea how naïve I sounded. "We live on an island down here in Pinehurst."

"No, we don't."

"Not a real one, but it might as well be," he said. "Life here between whites and blacks is different from most other places — especially different from the rest of the South."

"How's that?"

Dad sipped his drink and stared straight ahead. "Sure, you can't golf on Number 2...except when you play with Peter. And we're not even allowed to eat in town...like that all over the South no matter how far we get from the Civil War," he said. "But we can talk to white folk here and if we're respectful, we got no trouble."

"Got no trouble when I caddy," I said.

"You wouldn't," he said. "You do a good job. They appreciate it and do right by you. That's the way it's always been in Pinehurst. Yes, suh...come to Pinehurst and enjoy a slice of heaven – for a day, a week...maybe even the rest of your life. The Tufts tried to make Pinehurst a family place right from the start...employees and guests, all like one big family. You believe that, Son?"

"I do," I answered caught in the moment.

"Except we can't play golf here, can we?" he said, sipping at his vodka. "And the Jews can't play neither." He leaned into me. "But mark my words, Son, things are changing."

I could see the confusion on my face surprised Dad. He stood up – no stagger in his step – and glared at me. *"You can't see it?* I knowed it since I come back from the war. First old man Tufts died, then Ross couple of years later. Your friend, Richard Tufts, all alone now and he's come through some tough times...hell, a depression and a world war. Pinehurst hasn't seen good years since the '20s. Even Tufts is trying to call them last twenty years for Pinehurst 'the reorganization years.' *Reorganization*, hah! Rough years, that's all. But he knows things gotta change."

"But change how?"

Dad sat back down and leaned in close to me again. I could smell his breath, all hot, strong and sour from the booze. "Pinehurst, more than anything else, is a *business*. That's all it's ever been...that's how it survives."

"What you saying?"

"Well...pretty soon Pinehurst won't feel so much like a family," he said. "But you'll be able to play golf there and I don't mean just with Peter or in the Caddie Tournament."

That was my first real man-to-man talk with Dad...he was right, too. I learned a lot that night under our *Tree of Knowledge*. True enough — Pinehurst *was* an island. It was removed from the harsher segregation of the time. Maybe it was the influence of the Pinehurst "family" or maybe was just 'cause of it's being a resort town. Whatever the reason, it worked. Dad and his friends taught me how to appreciate people, all people, even the difficult ones...taught me how to enjoy their company. All Dad's friends were caddies one time or another. They knew the key to getting along was to treat people the same way you wanted them treating you. "We all come from Adam and Eve," they always told me. Really is just that simple, you know...the way we all should treat one another. Funny, how when things should be so simple, people just keep trying to make them so hard...

Now I learned *those* social graces well enough, but I guess I musta missed how best to socialize with the ladies, 'cause the next year I went and got a gal pregnant...wasn't even my girlfriend...was just a wild kid-fling. Anyway...had my first son, Jerry Goode...was 1953. A year after that, my true girlfriend, Alarrion, laid down the law. Guess you could say made me an officer and a gentleman 'cause she persuaded me to join the army. We got married right before I shipped out to Fort Jackson for basic training. But being so close to Pinehurst, I scurried home every chance I got and by the time I finished my stint, I had a daughter and another son on the way.

When I wasn't making babies, I was caddying at Pinehurst. One day I was walking over to the course when this white Cadillac sedan near sideswiped me right off the street. The man behind the wheel rolled down the window and hollered, "I need you today, Willie."

"Mr. Russell, how are you, suh?"

"Are you coming to caddy?"

"Most definitely."

"Good, you're my caddie."

"But, Mr. Russell, isn't —"

"No, he's not," O.V. Russell cut me off. "I need you. Now Willie, don't make this difficult," he added, wincing. "Since you went into the army, I'm down $10,000 to those jokers and I can't afford to be a penny more."

O.V. Russell owned a yarn factory in Troy, North Carolina and one thing he had was plenty of money. I knew he could afford to lose more...*a lot* more. But all I said was, "All right, Mr. Russell, I'll caddy for you."

"Great!" he replied with a smarmy grin as he peeled away in his car.

My step quickened. I felt all my nerves tighten in my body. This was the *Money Game*.

Far back as the 1930s, the likes of Tommy Armour and other Northeast PGA club pros would close shop for winter, pack up their golf clubs and head for sunny Florida. Back then there was just one way to get down the north/south corridor so they all took the same road, old Route 1. It was a long, tiring drive. Facilities were very few and far between, especially at the southern end. So they all looked forward to the one thing that made the trip bearable — a stopover in Pinehurst. Here for a few days, they'd play hard on the course by day and over at the old Dunes Club, where illegal gambling was always available, by night. Now Carl Andrews was the owner of the Dunes Club and was a real popular fella. He usually hosted the pros and even played with them in some mighty high stakes matches on Course Number 2.

But them money matches went on even when the pros weren't in town and I knew this one today would be a big one. If I was caddying for Mr. Russell, I knew he'd be up against Carl Andrews and sparks would fly sure enough. O.V.'s usual foursome was there, playing a $1,000 a hole, and none of that group took losing lightly.

Bags in tow, me and the other caddies reached the 1st tee. The players were already there waiting on us. Smiling big and toothy, Carl Andrews looked like he already had Mr. Russell's money in his pocket. North Lee Ray, he owned a clothing store in the village, had a smooth grin smeared on his face — so did Frank Stevenson, a millionaire several times over. They all knew Mr. Russell was having a bad patch with his game and they were all standing like vultures, ready to pick at the carcass. It wasn't losing the money that rankled them so much; it was the damage it done to their pride. Beating the other guy was all that mattered.

They never practiced first. "The game's out here," Mr. Russell told me once. "Not on the range." Soon as they spotted me, the competitive banter started up.

"Brought a ringer," Mr. Andrews snorted.

"Thought you were in the army, Willie. Even so, I'm afraid you can't help this guy win," Mr. Ray chided. "I think you've drawn a loser today, son."

"We'll see about that," Mr. Russell snarled before he parked his drive down the fairway, a good fifteen yards ahead of the others. "Son-of-a-bitch," he punctuated the drive as he strolled off the tee. He was a good player. I knew if I could crank up his confidence, he'd play some great golf. The best barometer for his game was not *what* he said, but *how* he said it. He could cuss good as anyone. Fact is, I think he knew more swear words than my dad and all his buddies combined – knew how to put them together, too. O.V. Russell had a big frame to go with his loud nature – a Panama hat and Cuban cigar woulda completed that picture just fine. The son-of-a-bitch phrase confirmed all was well.

Two of his three rivals reached the 1st green on their approach shots, but that didn't bother O.V. none. I handed him the 9-iron. He took it and stiffed the ball a foot shy of the hole. Couldn't help but smile at the string of curses that followed...it was downright musical.

"Stork City," I praised. He'd hit the ball stiff to the pin. I applauded as we padded to the green to register our 1st grand.

On the 2nd hole, Mr. Russell smoothed a 5-iron to within 5 feet. "Stork City," I chimed again. Two grand and we only been on the course some twenty minutes.

But this group didn't just play a $1,000 a hole. No suh. They went to automatic press if someone went two holes up. As we approached the 3rd tee, the press was on – it was double or nothing until someone won a hole. Mr. Russell waltzed to the tee calling out another rash of unrepeatables that golfers musta heard on the back 9. The louder and more enthusiastic those words slipped off his tongue, the angrier his rivals got. After O.V. striped another drive, I could just about see the steam pouring out of Mr. Stevenson's ears. He followed on the tee and pushed his drive well into the trees on the right.

His caddie, Jimmy Steed, tossed me a *Mona Lisa* look. Lengthy stretches of sand and wire grass flanked the fairways of Pinehurst Number 2 much as they do now. Out past those stretches ran rows of pine trees all surrounded by pine straw. Even so it's hard to lose a golf ball 'cause there ain't no real hazards like lakes or gnarly underbrush. Fact is I've heard it said Number 2 is the toughest course in the world *where you can't lose a golf ball.* So over the years, more than a few golfers have welcomed a little bit of *assistance.* Caddies would trudge off way ahead of their players just so they'd have time enough to *nudge* a ball that misbehaved...you know just kinda advance it to a more favorable lie. This way at least there'd be an opening for the next shot. Steed had to do that for Mr. Stevenson on the 3rd hole. That was the first nudge of the day for our foursome. Now the players knew he'd do it, but they wouldn't say nothing if they didn't see nothing. Even if they *did* see the ball suddenly squirt out of a bad lie, they most likely would just look the other way. There's a silent gentleman's agreement about golf-ball-nudging, and this well-tailored group respected it.

"You're making him play too damn good," Mr. Andrews snapped at me. "If you don't stop, I'm going to get someone to take you off this course."

He wasn't kidding neither and for the first time that day, I felt nervous.

"Leave my caddie alone," O.V. countered and it was game on. Mr. Russell had a simple three-quarter 9-iron for his approach to the 3rd. Sure enough...he drained the putt again. Up four grand now...I waited for the others to stomp off the green before I low whispered, "Stork City," to him.

"I heard that!" Mr. Andrews bellowed from the head of the pack and I felt my nerves tighten all over again.

The rest of the front 9 went peaceful enough...well...for this group anyway. Along with his $4,000. Mr. Russell added another grand for winning the front side Nassau. All us caddies added up the nudges: two for Mr. Andrews, three for Mr. Ray and just that one on the 3rd hole for Mr. Stevenson. *Not a one for my guy.*

We added two more nudges at the pesky right side of 11, but every man seemed to find his game after that. The only club giving Mr. Russell trouble was his 3-wood. Thing was most of the time this was a real good club for him — but not today. Unfortunately after he hit a mediocre drive on the long 14th, he needed it for his approach shot.

For the first time that day his string of cusses expressed irritation instead of pleasure. The others had waited a long time for this moment and they weren't about to let it pass. They needled him bad when they left the tee. So before he even reached his ball, he cracked, "Give me $5,000 if I make a three."

His partners erupted in a chorus of howls. My heart sank. This round had been so pleasant and now O.V. was just about to ruin it.

"How much will you give us?" North Lee Ray demanded.

"Are you kidding me?" Mr. Russell said. "The odds of me making a 3 are practically nil. 50-to-1."

"You're playing too good...2-to-1," countered Mr. Stevenson.

"Hah, you S.O.B.," my player cracked. "Okay, 5-to-1."

"You're on."

Now I had to break the bad news to Mr. Russell.

"Don't be telling me that, Willie," he hissed at me. "Don't be giving me the 3-wood."

"But, suh," I whispered back. "It's the only way you're going get there and give yourself a chance at a birdie."

"I haven't hit that blasted club all day."

"But you usually *do*," I shrugged. "It's *time*."

Glaring hard at me he took the dreaded club. There are times in a round when a caddie knows his tip's on the line. This was one of them. Up until now I was due a big one. But now I knew it all came down to this one shot. Should I say another word or just let him have at it?

I couldn't help myself. "Just think how sweet this 3 will be."

He smiled at that. Was only a thin kind of wry smile, but it was enough to settle him down some. He stood over that ball with more concentration, but not so much to paralyze him. No suh, he used just enough time to get real focused. Was worth it too...that was the best 3-wood he'd hit all day, maybe even the best of his life. It took flight straight, long and high, never wavered, then dropped softly inside 20 feet of the hole.

"Damn, what a shot!" he exclaimed to growls from the others.

But he still had to make the putt. I looked at that 15-footer from all angles. From behind it looked a little uphill. But I knew it wasn't. From the other side it looked a little downhill...*and that's what it was*. The sun leaned well left of noon so the grain would make the ball break just a bit more than usual.

"Play it two inches out to the right and don't hit it hard like you think you've got to," I said as I stepped away.

Still well focused, Mr. Russell curled the ball to the hole with perfection. It rattled in the cup to a new batch of unrehearsed curses along with a collection of groans from his rivals. I smiled...my hefty tip was safe and sound.

By the next hole the others were figuring O.V.'s luck would run dry, so they made a side bet with him that he couldn't make par. But when his tee shot snuggled just 8 feet from the hole, the cusses and groans that rose again were music to my ears. He purposely let his first putt roll to the hole and die millimeters from the lip...a tap-in par. They had their heads together on the next hole...probably trying to plot their last desperate bet against Mr. Russell. On the 17th tee, O.V. musta had the same thought 'cause he cut them short.

"Two pars will get me a 75," he announced. "Got any takers on that bet?"

Now the 17th and 18th holes on Number 2 are real challenging. You got a well- bunkered par 3 followed by a long uphill 4 par...O.V. normally had trouble with that last one.

"We'll take that bet," Mr. Stevenson barked while his buddies were still thinking it over.

I could see the others weren't so sure they wanted that bet but they all went along with Mr. Stevenson and took it anyway. O.V. plopped his tee shot into the bunker in front of the green. *Finally...*they could see a real crack in Mr. Russell's armor and they were ready to pounce. Just about giddy, Carl Andrews barked the newest challenge, "5-to-1 you can't get up and down from there."

"$1,000," Mr. Russell challenged him right back.

Mr. Andrews looked at the other two...they both nodded yes.

"I can't make it 1-in-5, but I can 1-in-10," O.V. noted his limitations. "You guys owe me a grand if I make it. If I don't, I owe you a $100...10-to-1."

"You're already up a bundle and a half," Mr. Andrews complained. "What more do you want?"

"T-E-N – To – O-N-E."

They took that bet but grumbled about it all the way to the green. Some days a player's just in the zone...happens with all golfers...the best and the worst. That day O.V. Russell was in the zone and the day belonged to him. Even when he looked vulnerable in a sand trap, he was still calling the shots. I pictured the shot in my mind even before he hit...he didn't disappoint. Sand and ball flew from the trap in a perfect arc. The ball skipped twice and stuck just as the name *Wilson* appeared. The ball lay only five inches south of the hole.

Mr. Russell, well, he didn't utter a word — he just basked in the volley of curses from his rivals. Still had to par the 18th, but the way he was playing I felt pretty confident he would. Not until he pulled his drive into the left rough did I start to worry. Those dreaded hooks usually get to a good golfer late in a round...and once they start, they're hard to shake.

"What do you think, Willie?" he asked me as we stood next to his ball.

He was a good 5-iron away but 'cause of the lie and his sudden suspect swing, I handed him the 6. He gave me a look like he knew it wasn't the right club, but he hit it anyway. Sure enough he pulled it left of the green and landed it in a bunker. This wasn't a green side trap neither. A Donald Ross golf course features tough greenside bunkers, but the master designer got real tricky when he created Number 2. Several traps sit ten to thirty yards from greens as well, and the bunker left of the 18th was one of those.

Was this another crack in the armor?

"5-to-1 you can't get up and down," Mr. Ray called out.

"10-to-1 and you're on," O.V. countered.

His chances were slim at best. Both that wager and the much bigger one of scoring 75 were on the line.

Mr. Andrews saw his chance. "Double or nothing on the 75 score and you're on."

Now O.V. knew it was a loaded bet...but he took it anyway...had no choice really.

My player took to the bunker with a 9-iron. He buried his feet like he was crushing a couple cartons of cigarettes and opened the blade of his club. Waggling, he dug deeper into the sand and cradled the 9-iron like he had a chicken by the neck. He took the club back a couple of times, careful not to graze the sand. When he finally hit, the explosion was one Bobby Jones himself woulda been proud to call his own. Shot like that shoulda had trumpets announcing it. The ball flew high in the air in its own shower of fluffy sand and landed with one hop a yard shy of the hole. *Incredible.*

Now some claim the chorus of cusses heralding that great shot was heard all the way to the village. That's probably not true, but I sure like to think it is. I only know my special wish for O.V. was that in his final moments before leaving this life, he recalled that fabulous moment on the 18th on Number 2, hurled one last string of cusses and felt the shower of money he won that day.

At Willie's invitation,
President Eisenhower finally arrives at Pinehurst.

CHAPTER SEVEN

GOLF'S A LUCKY CHARM AND HARRY TRUMAN

*M*y feet and legs are starting to get sore and kinda ache. Don't usually feel this way on a golf course. Makes me wonder how golfers find the energy to stand around at cocktail receptions after playing...

"So how much money did O.V. make that day?" someone asks.

"Can't quite recall," I reply. "I caddied for him every day that week."

"Did he ever lose?" another chirps.

"Not that week."

"How much did he win all together?"

"Don't know exactly. But it was a bunch," I say. "That week it was the same foursome every day, but I've caddied for that group when a few of the faces were different. They used to import some crazy wonderful people to play in those matches."

"Like who?"

"Dizzy Dean, the pitcher. Sammy Kaye, the band leader," I reply. "The betting was high so while the players were dressed in their finest tweeds, some of them had holes in their pockets."

Revelation of that old golf trick brought a ripple of laughter.

"Tell me," says a man in a black suit with red tie, "Did caddies really 'nudge' the ball back then?"

"What back then?" I answer. "Caddies still do."

Some look at me with concern, others nervously. I know which ones want a nudge or two a round and which ones don't.

"Now some golfers have holes in their pockets," I tell them. They look confused so I add, "When it looks like there's no hope of finding a ball, all of sudden one will come plopping out of the bottom of a pants leg, just like magic."

"I've seen that," I hear from somewhere in the crowd. Guess he was talking about a member of his foursome 'cause he added, "Bet that's how ol' Charlie saved that par from the woods!"

"You've caddied for a few presidents in your day, haven't you, Willie?" I'm asked.

"Four, to be sure."

A man wearing a navy blue pin-striped suit with a gold tie winks at me. "Did any of them have holes in their pockets?"

Now I had left high school at sixteen and by the time I was eighteen years old I was caddying in the 1951 Ryder Cup. Just three short years later, thanks to Alarrion, my long-time girlfriend from before I left high school, I found myself in the army.

"Willie don't you want to make something out of your life?" she challenged.

So marriage and the army followed in short order. Was fine by Alarrion that I joined the army...guess she figured her leash on me wouldn't stretch far enough unless we were married. Neither one of us realized it at the time, but as it turned out, our union not only kept me tied to her, but to Pinehurst, too. My career there as a caddie became that "something" I would make out of my life. I came home often on furloughs and spent most of my time on the links. I worked the big games with the O.V. Russell crowd, or...well as some much smaller ones...though can't rightly say I remember all those golfers. No matter the players, I always enjoyed the experience.

To this day, golf suits me right down to the ground. If I live to be a hundred, the game always will draw me to it. Whether I have a club in my hand or I'm handing one to another player, golf makes me tick...probably what's kept this life of mine going long as it has. Even when I was in the army, golf defined my time much more than the military ever did.

Not long after I signed up, I caddied for Major Charles James. He musta liked how I helped him around Number 2 because as he handed me a generous tip, he told me, "When you get to Fort Jackson for boot camp, look me up."

Only two days into boot camp I was missing golf something fierce so I decided to take the major up on his offer. Dressed in my new uniform, I marched into his outer office where his lieutenant aide stopped me forthwith.

"There's *no way* you're going to see Major James," the young officer said. "Soldier, you don't even know how to salute properly."

Looking through the doorway behind the lieutenant I could see the major working at his desk. The conversation in his front office broke his concentration and he looked up long enough to catch sight of me.

"I know that man, lieutenant," he called. "He was my caddie at Pinehurst. Send him in."

That poor lieutenant ended up being just the first in a tidy collection of officers whose toes I'd accidentally stepped on in the next two years...and all because of golf.

Major James rose with a warm, satisfied grin. He skipped the salute and shook my hand. "What took you so long to come see me?"

I lit up like a light bulb. This was the only real good thing that'd happened to me since I got to camp. "I shoulda done it sooner, suh."

"Damn straight," he confirmed. "Got your clubs?"

Was he kidding...golf in the army? "I didn't bring them."

The major couldn't believe what he just heard. His smile melted. *"What's the matter with you, man?"* He returned to his seat scowling. Social time definitely was over.

"Are you mad at me, sir?"

"Damn straight I am," he barked. "You need to get yourself a pass, go home and get those clubs."

No need to tell me twice. Problem was when I asked my company commander for a pass, he thought I was arrogant, crazy, or both. "You've been here *three* days, soldier. I'm not giving you no damn pass!"

"He wouldn't, huh," Major James noted when I returned to his office. "I've already told the brass around here that you were going home to get your clubs this weekend. Damn. We'll just see about that – here." Without another word, he'd written a pass and handed it to me just as simple as can be. "Forty-eight hours. Be back here by 1100 hours Sunday."

So golf had become my lucky charm...it overrode the wrath of my commander and got me a pass home. Alarrion was both surprised and happy to see me home so soon, but I knew she musta been disappointed in the long run 'cause I was on a mission; getting my golf clubs and getting back on time was all that mattered. But then my luck seemed to go bad because the train from Southern Pines to South Carolina was late that Sunday morning. It didn't pull into the North Carolina station until 10:48, less than twenty minutes away from my reporting deadline.

But I was soon to discover that golf's good luck charm still rode my shoulder...fact be known it was my bag full of clubs that saved me. There I sat in uniform, flower sack between my knees, all the while fretting my tardiness and its consequences, when an officer wearing fatigues and a star strolled down the aisle of the train car. He stopped, duffel bag in hand. His bulldog face towered over me. My eyes met his and I fumbled to stand up.

"Stay seated, soldier," he told me. "You going to Fort Jackson?"

"Yes, suh," I stuttered, knowing the trouble I was in.

"You're going to be late."

"I know, suh, but —"

He cocked his head. "Major James sent you home to get your clubs, didn't he?"

"Yes, suh. I can expl —"

"Smart move," the general noted. "You did your golfing at Pinehurst, no?"

"Yes, suh."

"Major James told me."

"Yes, suh."

"From what he told me, you play well, Son."

"Major's heard about my playing is all, but thank you, suh." I was afraid to say anything more. I was still thinking about all the trouble I was in.

Him studying and standing over me like that just was making me more and more nervous by the second. "Mind if I sit down?"

"Of course not, suh." Imagine that, a general asking to sit next to *me* on a train. The army sure enough was an unusual place. Clubs still between my legs, I slid across the seat to make room. When I looked back at the general, I was surprised to find he was wearing a big warm smile.

That man made the trip to South Carolina pass by real quick...told me he'd fought with black soldiers in the past. "Give me a group of Negro soldiers and I can win any war," the general told me. I don't think he was lying, not the way he said it. By the time we arrived, he'd invited me to caddy for him. "Don't worry about being late today," he said as we approached his waiting car. The guard at the gate didn't hesitate a second — just waved us on through. When he left me at my barracks, he rolled down the window and said goodbye. There was no doubt about who was dropping me off. I know my company commander musta come up with more than one nasty punishment for my tardiness, but he never found the nerve or the opportunity to follow through with any of them. When I told him what'd happened, all he said was, "You rode back with *General Collins?*" A short time later the commander got shipped overseas and I got made me the number one golfer on the Fort Jackson squad.

By then I'd learned to play pretty good golf and had a couple of tournaments under my belt...but I'll save all that for later...only mention it here 'cause my skill level let me keep some strong company in the army. Major James saw to it that I met all the brass who spent as much time on the golf course as they could. I gave lessons to captains and generals and a few full birds in between. Before long they asked me to play a round or two with them and I saw how easy golf smoothed out everything for me with both race and rank.

But my dream-like stint crashed and burned one day when I opened that letter. I'd survived boot camp, so according to the army, I was ready for the real world, well...Iceland, anyway. The name alone told me I'd be putting away the clubs for a long, long time. Sitting on the side of my cot, I read my orders. Alarrion was pregnant with our first child. Here I'd never been farther from Pinehurst than Georgia and now I was going to some island in the Atlantic to freeze for a few years.

"Hey, Willie," my buddy, Charlie Cameron, called to me from the barrack's door. "Major James wants to see you on the double."

Didn't need telling twice...just the sound of that man's name was comfort to me. The major had been there for me every step of the way up until now. I suddenly found myself praying he could make Iceland go away.

But I never imagined hearing, "Willie, I'm being reassigned to Fort Dix," when I entered his office. I panicked but then saw his smile was full of mischief. He stood there grinning a moment then added, "And you're going with me."

"But, suh, I'm going to Iceland."

He just smiled even wider, "Golf will be better in New Jersey."

The major had my orders changed just as easy as he wrote me that pass the first week of camp. I wasn't assigned to his direct charge but might as well have been. Just like he did at Fort Jackson, Major James took me under his wing and introduced me around to the Fort Dix brass. Golf's lucky charm was still riding my shoulder and helping me through army life.

"This is a good man from Pinehurst," he'd say. "And he sure knows his golf."

Once or twice a week, I played with colonels and generals, a $10 Nassau each time. No matter how they paired me, they never beat me. I was kinda embarrassed about taking their money, but they never seemed to mind. Besides, I had a pregnant wife and every little bit helped. Fact is they paid me some for lessons, too, so it occurred to me that maybe I should turn pro when I left the service.

Harry S. Truman

I shot a 73 the day they asked me to caddy for President Truman. The retired leader was coming to Fort Dix for some conference that soldiers of my rank knew little to nothing about.

"You're the unanimous choice," Major James announced, beaming..."Since you're a caddie at the greatest course in the United States."

"Choice for what, suh?"

I was standing at ease in the major's office as he was leaning real casual like up against his desk.

"Willie, we want you to caddy for President Truman."

A president...I'd lugged bags for some great people, impressive golfers, but never for a president.

"Why yes, suh," I replied with a wide smile. "Don't I just always get the tough duty? Who else will be in the foursome?"

He glared at me. "Does it matter?"

Why didn't he want to tell me? I thought maybe it was 'cause he wasn't sure or maybe it was 'cause he just didn't care for me asking the question...couldn't tell.

"You know them," he told me.

Two generals and a colonel — I'd taken money from all of them...and from one of the generals just last week.

Found out real quick there was no need to be nervous neither. I soon learned the former president was a gentleman in every sense of the word. There'd be no holes in the pockets of his foursome and heaven help the caddie who nudged a ball *this* day. Best of all...*President Truman was mine for the next four hours.* Funny how he didn't strike me like a politician...he asked me questions and actually listened to what I had to say. Maybe since he'd slipped back to his home in Missouri, he'd been able to shed politics and become a normal human being again. He wasn't the type of man I'd ever picture as leader of the whole United States. He was a gentleman, true enough, but had a chip or two, and was kinda rough around the edges...oh, not in a negative way, more cordial like, you know, friendly. He loved cracking a joke and treated everyone with respect...put us at ease. He made all us caddies feel like we were more than ordinary men and that made him all the greater in our eyes. For me his roughness defined him and gave him the character of an honest man, someone who embraced so much of life that he'd fit in anywhere and everywhere, Pinehurst or Taylortown. I decided right then and there that President Truman would make anyone a fine neighbor.

"I hear you come from Pinehurst," he said as we strolled down the second fairway. "That you caddied there."

"Well, suh, I'm really from a place near it called Taylortown," I replied. "Grandpa has a farm there and we all work it."

"A farm, huh," the president said. "I grew up on a farm too, my grandpa's same as you."

I gazed at him. Learning I'd started the same way as a president made me feel privileged. "When I turned 10, Dad made me start caddying — to make more money 'cause of the war."

"That so," he said. "Growing up, I worked as a timekeeper on the Santa Fe Railroad. I slept in a hobo camp. Know what that is?"

I shook my head.

"That's where people with no money sleep," he told me. "Migratory workers."

Don't that beat all? Growing up I'd actually had it *better* than him.

"Count your blessings, Son," he said, sizing me up. "Wish *I* worked on a golf course when I was 10."

I learned a lot about this president before the round ended. He'd said he envied *me* and *he had been the top man in the land*!

"Have you ever been to Pinehurst, suh?"

He nodded. "Nice place." He studied me 'gain. "I hear you learned a thing or two about this game down there."

I smiled and raised my eyebrows but didn't say a word.

"Have you been playing long?"

"Since I started caddying."

He seemed surprised. "Where did you get a set of clubs when you were 10?"

"I started out with just one club."

"Someone give it to you?"

"No, suh. I went into the woods, cut down a blackjack —"

"A what?"

"A blackjack, suh," I told him. "A small oak tree...I sanded down the root of it until it felt smooth like the face of a club. Cut it down to size, wrapped tape around the top for a grip and had myself a right fine driver."

He seemed impressed and measured my accomplishment with a widening smile.

"See anything in my game that needs improving?"

Was he serious? The shocked look on my face musta betrayed my thoughts 'cause he said, "I've had a double bogey on the 1st hole and would not like to have another one anytime soon. So be honest."

Like I said, the president struck me to be an honest man and honest men know when you're lying. "I *have* noticed a thing or two," I ventured.

I saw a number of things I could have mentioned, but I knew good pros focused on only one or two at a time. More than that could be disastrous to a man's game especially if you tell him during a round.

"Well, Son, help me out here. Give me some pointers."

"Your grip, sir," I said as we walked down the fairway. I didn't think the generals would much like me monopolizing the president so I decided to be quick. "Your grip's too strong."

I thought that was all I had to say.

"Strong, how?" asked the former president.

Still walking, I pulled a club from his bag and held it out in front of me. "You're left hand is like this," I told him, "with all your knuckles showing. You need to move your left hand to where that V is more on top of the club, and let your right hand move left, like this."

I ended up with a neutral grip on the club and glanced at President Truman. He seemed genuinely intrigued and when he lined up for his next shot, he wrestled with his fingers trying to duplicate my grip.

"It feels funny," he said. "I hold the club the way I do so I'll stop the big fade. So I'll hook it."

"But you don't hook, do you, suh?"

"No, I don't."

"It's because you're blocking each shot, pushing it right."

"I'll be damned," he said before striking the ball straight at the green. "I'll be damned."

I tried to stop there but after the president parred the 2nd, he was anxious for more. My advice buoyed his already friendly mood, which pleased his playing partners.

"Willie, tell him other stuff if that's what he wants," whispered one of the generals as we approached the 3rd tee.

So then on the 4th hole I told Harry Truman to loosen up his right hand...no more...just that.

On the 5th hole I told him to keep his left arm a tad straighter, which he did. Even presidents, I learned that day, can make good students.

On the 6th hole, after a crooked shot into the trees on the right, I swore to myself that this would be the last lesson I'd give the man.

But then I found myself saying, "Don't bring the club too much inside," anyway.

The last shot had irritated the president. I could hear it in his snapped response. *"What?"*

"Too much inside on your back swing," I said. "It's causing you to loop at the top and cut across the ball. Here, I'll show you." I put his golf bag down and took out a 7-iron. As I took the club back slowly, I said, "See how the club and my arms start out away from my body?"

He nodded, frowning hard the whole time he watched.

Now I had an audience — two generals, a colonel and two other privates who were made caddies for the day.

"And it comes back as I turn," I continued as I kept taking the club back. "I don't wrap it around my body. You do that and the club gets stuck — forces you to loop when you come back. Get it, suh?"

Total silence and a range of looks from baffled to annoyed greeted my explanation. I'd given one too many instructions. This was a point meant to be made on a driving range, not here. But the president was up for trying the new move. I'm not quite sure how he did it, but he shot near 80 that day. When he managed to stay in the fairway, he played good and woulda scored even better but for a handful of some real wild shots.

After the round he put his arm around my shoulders. No handshake from this man. "I'm coming to Pinehurst, Willie. And when I do, I want you on my bag."

"It'll be an honor, suh," I told him.

He came to the village, though, not when I was there. That's probably just as well...caddying for him that one time was a unique experience and one I still treasure. If you can't caddy for God, caddying for the President of the United States is the next best thing.

*About President Gerald Ford, legendary entertainer
Bob Hope once quipped, "You don't know what fear is
until you hear Ford behind you shouting, 'Fore!' —
and you're still in the locker room."*

CHAPTER EIGHT

MORE ROUNDS WITH PRESIDENTS

"You've got to be kidding, Willie," says the man in the red tie. "That isn't true."

"But it is," I tell him.

Others join in. They're all fascinated by my Truman story. Probably all the men standing around me make more money than Harry Truman ever did, but you can see they're plum tickled about me rubbing elbows with the closest thing we have to royalty in the United States – a president. My experience with presidents through the years has helped me understand how little difference there really is between men from different walks of life. But having all these suits gape in awe and hit me with such simple kinds of questions makes me realize many men don't realize that basic truth.

"Did he really shoot that well?"

"What did the generals think about all this?"

"How can any man learn how to change his swing as much as that with just a few pointers?"

"To tell the truth, I told him too much for one round," I reply. "I thought sure I'd screw up his game but good." I shake my head.

"But I didn't...Like I said, he listened to what I had to say, and tried what I told him...Just tells me, no one's too good to learn a thing or two."

"Other presidents?" the gold tie pipes up. "Ever caddy for any other presidents?"

"Two others," I answer. "No...forgot about Richard Nixon...make it three."

"See that," quips plaid shirt and tie. "So many he can't remember them all."

Dwight David Eisenhower

President Eisenhower was fond of sports — all sports, but most especially golf. The president had played with everyone at the time and everyone seemed to want to play with him. Once he even tangled with a tree on the 17th hole of Augusta National. He ended up losing that one...well, that's how I heard it. Anyway the incident got talked about so much they ended up naming that tree after him.

Back then Fort Dix held a winter parade every year and in 1955 President Eisenhower came to attend. True to form, he wanted to meet the players on all the post teams — baseball, football, and of course, golf. I was captain of the team just like I was at Fort Jackson and Major James had arranged a luncheon so the president could meet all the players.

Now President Eisenhower met with all the players from the different teams, but he saved lunch just for the golfers.

"It's great to be here, boys," he told us.

We were in awe of the man, not just because he was president...

needless to say that was something special in itself...but for us army guys it was unbelievable that we were standing there talking to the main military guy in World War II. His war credentials meant more to us than anything else.

President Eisenhower looked around and surveyed the five tables surrounding his. They were all full of brass smiling big toothy grins.

"You fellas are doing a great job. That's really what I came here to say. But being the fan I am, I want to know how you're doing *off* the drill field. Where's the team's captain?" I raised my hand and he asked, "What's your name, Son?"

"Willie McRae, suh."

"I hear you know a thing or two about golf."

"Yes, suh," I replied. "Guess they wouldn't have made me team captain if I didn't."

That drew a chuckle or two and another smile from the president. "What was your best score?" he asked.

"Sixty-four, suh."

"Great score. Where did you shoot that?"

"Right here, suh."

"Where do you come from, soldier?"

"Pinehurst...well actually next door...Taylortown."

"You learned to play golf at Pinehurst?"

"No, suh. I caddy there mostly," I told him. "But I've shot 70 on Number 2."

"You don't say. When was *that?*"

"During a caddie tournament, suh."

"Ah, I see. I hear Pinehurst's a great place."

"Yes, suh, sure is," I replied proudly. Guess I musta answered a little *too* proudly 'cause my answer brought a roll of muffled laughter.

"I've always wanted to play Number 2," he said. "You think if I ever get down that way you could arrange a game for me?"

My eyes widened. "Absolutely, Mr. President...you just say when."

One year later my tour was up. During the last game I played with the generals, they asked me to stay on and become the base golf pro. I was flattered...but while I enjoyed my time there, I missed home and my family more. The brass was pretty disappointed that I declined to stay on, but they understood why I needed to leave.

And so I returned to Pinehurst...hadn't been back very long when Richard Tufts invited President Eisenhower to come down and play. I double-looped for them both and my friend, Hilton Rogers, caddied for the opposing twosome, Peter Tufts and the then current president of Pinehurst Resort. Before we started out, 10 or 12 Secret Service, all wearing curly wires stuck in their ears, took to the links, stretched themselves out along the 1st fairway and halfway down the second, and tried to look inconspicuous. I remember two people came onto the course from across the street to maybe catch a glimpse of the president, but they were ushered off the course — pretty rudely, too!

I wasn't altogether sure how to deal with Eisenhower the golfer. Oh, make no mistake, President Eisenhower was an avid golfer, but I just couldn't forget he was the commander-in-chief. I been out of the army only a short time and the military hierarchy was still playing in my mind. Caddying for the boss of all the generals was downright intimidating. I suddenly felt nervous so I decided to stay a step behind him all the way down the 1st fairway of Number 2.

"Willie, what are you doing *back there?*" he said as we approached the green. "I didn't come here just for my health. If I'm going to make it through this round, you're going to have to help me, especially on these greens."

I smiled. "Yes, suh, these here greens are some of the hardest on earth, suh."

"How long have you been caddying here?"

"Near fifteen years, suh."

"Then I know you know how to read these greens."

"You bet I do, suh," I said. "But we best get to the greens before I read one for you."

He laughed as we stood twenty yards left of the 1st green. It took him two shots to get to the putting surface and three putts to find the hole. He seemed disgusted, maybe even just a little discouraged, but I saw a couple of things we could work on that just might save his round.

On the 2nd tee he hooked his drive dangerously close to Midland Road.

"What am I doing *wrong*, Willie?" he asked in a tone demanding a response.

"Suh, you're straightening your right arm too much."

"That's it?"

"It makes you come over the top of the ball," I explained. "Relax that arm and bring the club back slower. That should do it, suh."

And sometimes it did...but even try like he did, the president found himself fighting that nagging duck hook the whole day. As for the greens, reading them would be the easy part...the hard part was going to be grooving his putting stroke and working on his short game.

"Mr. President, you like to peek on those chip shots, don't you?" I asked after he stubbed his third chip in two holes. "Play the ball back three or four inches, so it's just about back to the big toe of your right foot."

"Like this?" he asked as he moved the ball back. "Around here?"

"Good, suh," I said. "Now you can hit the ball *before* you look up."

"Give me another ball." I handed him one and he declared, "I've got to try this."

He dropped the ball and set it well back in his stance. "Boy, this feels strange. I'm not sure."

"Just try it, suh."

"Am I *too* close to the ball?"

"About ten inches foot-to-ball is good."

"That *close*, huh?"

"Trust me, suh," I tried to reassure him. "Now stroke it like you stroking a long putt."

He did and the ball flew about ten yards, landed on the green and rolled out six or seven feet from the hole. "I'll be dammed," he exclaimed, surprised by his own success. I chuckled to myself. Bet he didn't know Mr. Truman had that same reaction to his own improvement just couple years before. Guess even presidents get caught and tickled by surprises.

I decided to deal with President Eisenhower's putting on the 5th green 'cause that green is *always* a fierce challenge. The president had a jerky motion to the ball almost like he was afraid of putting...you know, like he just wanted to get it over with soon as possible. Fear can hit the best of putters on Number 2's crowned greens, and the putt Mr. Eisenhower was about to attempt was as difficult as any on the course. The 5th green is fairly normal on the right side where his ball sat, but now he had to putt to the treacherous left front, a downhill curler of about 25 feet. The pin rested on the crest of the false front making the shot especially treacherous. *Oh Lord now today of all days, why did maintenance decide to put that pin there?*

"Mr. President, hit it soft like it's only a five-footer," I coached. "And don't move your head."

He obeyed like a private taking a command. Unfortunately the ball died on the crest of the false front, making his second putt even harder...straight down the hill.

"Now what?" he asked.

Hilton Rogers tossed me a "good luck" smirk.

It *was* the most God-*awful* putt to attempt. Just looking at that ball cross eyed would get it sliding down the hill past the pin and off the green to a yawning bunker.

I tried to prepare the president. "Suh, you have to understand that this putt is near impossible. I haven't seen but one person *ever* make it from where you are."

Knew I made a mistake soon as the words left my mouth...to this day don't know why I said what I did...if the man's already afraid of putting, this twister would cramp him up sure.

"Tap it, sir," I said.

Problem was Mr. Eisenhower musta heard me say "rap" instead of "tap" 'cause that ball just took off. It flew, zipping down the hill, hopped strong over the powerless rough and scurried right into the jaws of the hungry waiting trap.

"Pick it up," the president ordered, as him and the others took off for the 6th tee.

The president didn't ask me for any more help and I didn't offer him none. Instead we talked about our stints in the army. Imagine comparing my two years of duty with his famous career — his profound impact on warfare. Even though comparing the two showed real plain the distance between us in experience, he was just as interested in my puny uneventful stint as I was in his long historical one. He seemed settled in his game again by time we reached the back 9.

President Eisenhower three-putted the 10th. On the way to the 11th — Hogan's birdie hole — he said, "Willie, I wish you'd help me with my putting."

Instantly I recalled the debacle at the notorious 5th. "No problem, suh."

"Well, what do you think I'm doing wrong?"

I was reluctant to say what I *really* thought...but he'd asked for it. I took a deep breath and offered, "Mr. President, it's like...well...it's like you're *afraid* of putting.

He frowned. Standing right in front of me was one of America's greatest warriors and here I was telling him he was scared of something...much less something like putting. He didn't answer right off. Instead he gave me a look made me think if I was back in the army, he woulda court martialed me sure.

"*Afraid...*" I'll never forget the way he got his mouth around that word, and uttered it like that word was from another language, and he had to practice it before he could let anyone else hear it.

"*Afraid,* how?" was all he asked.

"Well, suh, you're real quick," I ventured as I set down his bag, "Like you want to get the putt done fast as you can instead of waiting to hear the ball rattle in the cup."

"Interesting," he pondered. "How do I change that, Willie?"

"Well, suh, you've got to keep your head still for starters," I said. "You move your head on every putt."

"I've heard that before."

"Keep your head down and still until you hear the ball a rattling." I was on a roll. "And, suh, it'll rattle a time or two."

He nodded. "I think I can do that."

Turned out, he did it just fine. For the remaining eight holes, he didn't three putt once and sunk a 12-footer on the 16th green for par.

President Eisenhower wasn't the most accomplished golfer of the presidents I caddied for, but he *was* the most avid. Beneath that grandfather exterior and warm genuine smile was the heart of a lion. When he missed a shot, he was hard on himself. He shot around 90 that day and probably never would do much better than that. But his competitive nature and disciplined background would never let him settle for disappointment. He wanted to shoot in the 70s and he'd try like hell to do it before he'd ever quit.

I thoroughly enjoyed my brief time with the commander-in-chief and if I'd been in World War II like Dad, I woulda been proud to serve under him.

Gerald R. Ford

President Ford came to Pinehurst twice...the first time to inaugurate the World Golf Hall of Fame in 1974, and the second time 19 years later, to help launch the resort's Centennial Golf Course, Pinehurst Number 8. As a warm-up to his ceremonial round at Number 8, him and Byron Nelson took on Number 2. I was lucky enough to be on the president's bag. Hilton Rogers caddied for Mr. Nelson. The event included a slew of Secret Service agents wearing wires in their ears, moving strategically from hole-to-hole while the golfers played.

President Ford and Mr. Nelson came out of the clubhouse like men on a mission. A large man, the president moved real deliberate, like he was trying to conceal sports injuries he'd got in his younger years. Byron Nelson, his sagging jowls starting to betray his age...still had a swagger in his step that made it crystal clear his flexibility was good as ever. To my surprise, Hardrock Robinson, now retired from caddying, was walking right along with the president.

"The man handed me $100 just because *he* knew *my* name," Robinson told me before we started the round. "Said he heard I was a legend here so he gave me the money. *Can you believe that?!* Treat him well, Son, and you'll make a big tip – $100. *WOW*...makes me feel obliged to follow you guys around the course today."

I doubt if there coulda been a better pairing for that day. Two men with vastly different careers, and both of them perfect gentlemen –

they carried their grand experience real quiet like in their pockets, didn't wear it loud and screaming on their sleeves. They treated Hilton and me so good at times it felt like we were caddying for friends instead of the closest thing this country has to royalty. They introduced themselves to us even though we knew who they were...and it wasn't no brush-off kind of introduction neither. They shook our hands and introduced themselves by name. The way they chatted us up was like America was no bigger than Pinehurst Number 2...wanted to know our names and where we come from. From the way they listened to our answers, I think they musta remembered us for a good long while afterwards too. Now maybe they were just killing time before that ceremonial round the next day, but I think they were happy to escape the rules and regulations of their normal routines. I got the feeling Gerald Ford especially understood poor folks. He was an outright man, reminding me some of President Truman, you know, honest like he didn't know how to be no different. Walking and talking around the course with him made me wonder whatever made a man like him go off and be a politician.

Now with Byron Nelson for his playing partner, I wasn't about to give the president advice about his game. Fact is, most of the day I just watched Mr. Nelson play. What a nice smooth swing — like he was born to play the game. Hilton would hand him a club and Mr. Nelson would let it rip. Like all great golfers, his swing was the same every time. His swing was so good and so consistent, they even named the mechanical machine that tests golf clubs after him...called it the "Iron Byron." Some say that he had the best swing ever, and that if all the greats of the game had got to play tournaments together, he woulda won most of them. No wonder when he was up against the likes of Hogan and Snead, Nelson won eleven tournaments in a row.

"How do you think I'm doing, Willie?" the president asked me on the 3rd hole.

"You got a good game, suh."

"No, not my *game*," he kinda chuckled. *"How am I doing in Washington?"*

"Oh, I think you're doing a good job there, too, suh," I said with a huge grin. "And keep on doing it!"

He laughed. "I can only do as much as Congress will let me," he said.

"Well, keep plugging, suh."

He liked that and I remember we had a good time cruising around the course. On the treacherous 5th green he putted the ball on the line I gave him and it wound its way to stop just an inch from the cup. "How can you be so good at reading these greens, Willie?" he asked. "I never would have seen that much break."

"If you been out here long as I have, suh," I replied, "You *better know* these greens."

He nodded. "Makes sense..."

"Like your job, suh," I went on. "You know how to do your job and I sure don't. I rely on you to do your job, Mr. President, and you rely on me to do mine."

He played pretty consistent and never really asked me for any advice. Someone like that, I wasn't about to volunteer any. Instead he wanted to talk about life. We musta sounded almost philosophical when we started talking about how everyone had a job to do and

Byron Nelson – the man with the near perfect swing

how everyone's contribution, no matter how small it might seem, was for the good of the country.

"How did you get into caddying?" he asked me as we strutted down the 11th fairway.

"Well, suh, Dad caddied and figured I should too."

"Do you like it?"

"You bet, suh," I answered. "If you don't like your job, I think you should give it up and stop wasting time that's all too short to start with. Don't you agree, suh?"

He frowned mulling over my last statement. Had I put my foot in my mouth? Just then it hit me...deciding on whether or not you like being a caddie, a trash collector or even a lawyer is one thing...but once you get to be president, it can't be so easy to quit if you decide you don't like the job. I had mixed an apple with my oranges, but just as I realized what I done, Mr. Ford's expression softened.

"You're right, Willie," he said. "But still, no matter what it is we do, everyone is somebody for doing it."

"You're right too, suh," I told him with a big grin. No matter what political party you favor, how could you not like Gerald Ford?

As we trudged on up the 18th hole, I could see his old football injuries slowing his stride some. "I think I'll have to find time to come back here," he said.

"Why not, suh?" I chimed in. Then without thinking who this man was, I quipped, "Such good looking women you think you've come to the wrong place."

As he laughed, I wondered how many presidents I could have

used that line with. Gerald Ford gave me $150 dollars for my time and for that 81 he shot.

"I think I *will* come back," he said. "Everyone has been so nice to me."

Hardrock Robinson had walked all 18 holes with us. He looked at me wide-eyed, surprised by the president's comment. "Mr. President, of course we treat you right," he broke in. "And not just 'cause you're a generous man neither; we treat you right 'cause you *deserve* it."

Richard M. Nixon

Caddied once for President Nixon but frankly my memory of the round is too fuzzy to recall all the details...I *do* remember he could play and hit the ball a long way...scored real respectable that day, too...high 70s as I remember. His two birdies late in the round eased the hurt of his double bogey start along with several other bogies. He seemed real pleased with himself and spread his joy around so to speak...treated me and the others real good. But I honestly think he woulda done the same even if he shot 99. Now maybe some might think he acted that way 'cause he was first and foremost a politician, but I like to think it was 'cause he was just a good man at heart. I remember his staff was real fond of him...said he treated everyone with respect and consideration.

Man like that always manages to shorten that bridge between him and the rest of us...for my money Richard Nixon was one more president who did just that.

Willie "On The Bag" with Chi Chi Rodriguez

CHAPTER NINE

MEMORABLE MOMENTS WITH GOLFING GREATS

"*Willie, those stories about the presidents are quite something,*" *says the man in the gold power tie.* "*But the '60s were a wild decade... the Vietnam War, hippie protests at the Pentagon, the Kennedy assassination...*"

"*And civil rights,*" *inserts another suit from back of the group.*

"*Yeah, how did Pinehurst handle all that?*" *asks the paisley brown tie.*

Wasn't expecting questions like that...they kinda catch me off guard so I hesitate a bit. "*Didn't really have too many problems like that at the resort. Golfers — mostly all well-to-do like y'all — well, they were just interested in getting good caddies that could help them around the course. They treated us according to our abilities to do that.*"

"*What do you mean?*" *asks a man I don't remember seeing before now. He's wearing a yellow tie.*

"*Guess it's like with any job, you gotta know how to do it and do it right,*" *I answer.* "*With my job...you gotta know the greens, how to find balls and read the wind. Gotta club your guy right, too* *if you honestly gonna help your man around the course. You do that and your golfer will do right by you...it's pretty much a two-way street out there. But if you're there just to tote his bag, **watch out**. There a bunch of guys out there looking to get away with doing little as they can...but they don't last long."*

"So you led a blessed life in Pinehurst?" asks paisley tie. "Racially speaking, that is."

I reflected for a moment. "Never had a problem where I lived...Taylortown...white folk used to come visit our place and we visited theirs. We all helped each other out in the fields, too. Black and white worked side-by-side 'cause we were neighbors. Of course, the white kids had to go to Pinehurst for schooling and we stayed in Taylortown."

The group stays quiet, looking to me for more. "We were treated good but we knew our place, so to speak."

"But you lived in the South in the '60s," notes another newcomer.

I nod with a wry smile. "Oh, I met the clan once or twice. Once a guy with a hood on his head came up to me, got in my face and told me he was gonna burn a cross on my land. I guess some fellas feel real tough when you can't see their faces."

"What did you do?" asks yellow tie.

"Told him I'll burn one on your ass...and I didn't need no hood to tell him neither!"

"What did he do then?" asks the black and red tie.

"He left. Bullies always do when you challenge them," I answer with a wink. "Caddying helped a lot to get around the segregation

issue. A golfer and a caddie gotta work as a team if that golfer's gonna succeed. A good golfer respects a good caddie and vice versa. Back then golfers at Pinehurst were white, caddies were black...just the way it was...didn't have many problems. Fact is, I had to leave golf for a while to really feel prejudice."

Gold tie speaks up. "Tell us about that."

"Wait," cuts in another. "I want to hear more about the great players you caddied for."

"Tell you what," I answer. "I'll tell you a bit about both."

The 1960s were turbulent times for the nation so they managed to turn Pinehurst upside down along with everything else. By then Richard Tufts had reached the age where he wanted to retire and spend most of his time playing golf and reminiscing about the good old days. Was a sad time when he lost his wife...but then he remarried in 1964 and couple years later his former son-in-law, James Harrington, became President of Pinehurst. He disagreed with Mr. Richard (that's what I came to call Mr. Tufts) about the direction the resort should take. Mr. Richard wanted to preserve the family tone of a small town in the South. But Mr. Harrington...well now he thought only development and real change could help Pinehurst survive since new resorts, like Hilton Head in South Carolina, were starting to give ol' Pinehurst a run for its money. So the new president started stepping to the beat of his *own* drum. He went around Mr. Richard and got support from Mr. Richard's brothers, Albert and James. That's how on a cold day in December 1970, James Harrington wiped out family tradition and sold the resort to

Malcolm McLean for 9.2 million dollars. Pinehurst Resort became
Pinehurst, Incorporated...part of the holding company Diamondhead.

Now earlier in that decade I was privileged to caddy for Hugh
Stewart. Mr. Stewart was a member of Pinehurst and owned a few
oil wells up in Ohio. He used to go back and forth from Pinehurst
to there like it was a normal rush-hour commute. Sadly, an
automobile accident cut short his golfing. The poor man had to have
his leg amputated. A little after his recovery, he sought me out
because he wanted me to be his chauffeur. Mr. Stewart was a good
man...always had done right by me. Thought about it and figured
since I been caddying for quite some time, maybe I was ready for
something different and decided to take the job. So on 21 November
1963, the day before President Kennedy was shot, I became Mr.
Stewart's driver.

We drove up to Ohio real regular and I developed a strong bond
with the man. I still can recall this one time we were in the Tin
Whistles room of the Pinehurst Clubhouse. The Tin Whistles...good
group of people...been supporting golf in Pinehurst for as long as I
can remember. Anyway I was sitting outside the open-door room
while my boss and a group of men were inside playing poker. Mercer
Hufford, owner of the Manor Hotel in town, got all mad about some
hand.

"Damn it, Hugh," he snarled. "You do a thing like that again and
I'll jump on that broke leg of yours."

I bolted to my feet, stormed into the room and stared down the
hotel owner. "You hit my boss," I growled, "and you're gonna have
one very bad day."

Well Mr. Stewart thought it best for us to leave, so he quit the card game...but that small smile at the corner of his mouth told me he liked what I said.

That's the kind of relationship we had — I had his back and he had mine. We ate in the same restaurants and slept in the same hotels. When the owner of the hotel where we used to stay in Ohio came to visit Pinehurst I was happy to caddy for him...he was a good man. Fact is never had a problem anywhere in Ohio...but now West Virginia...that was a different story. First time we stopped to eat, they refused to serve me. Mr. Stewart told them, "The money that pays for Willie pays for me as well...if that money's not good enough to pay for him, then it's not good enough to pay for me either."

And we left. I knew Mr. Stewart was hungry. I told him I woulda eaten out back, but he said it was the principle of the thing.

Then this one trip I had the feeling Mr. Stewart wasn't doing too good. We were cruising through West Virginia when he told me, "Willie, we just have to stop. I'm famished."

I pulled over. It wasn't the same restaurant like before, but we got the same reception.

"Your man can't eat in the dining room," the greeter said at the door. "He has to eat in the back room."

Mr. Stewart wanted to protest the way he did before, but I knew he was tired and hungry plus I was worried he was feeling ill. So before he could open his mouth I blurted, "It's *okay,* suh. I'll eat out back."

He wasn't happy about it but he let me go. Turns out that room was actually okay...didn't smell bad and even had pictures hanging on one wall. I sat there surrounded by quiet and thought about how good the food was. I'm sure it was the same food they were serving Mr. Stewart in the dining room. He was right...same money paid for us both...and we probably were enjoying the same chicken and corn. I was sure that's what he was eating too 'cause when we were together in Ohio we ate that more often than not. So here we were eating the same meal, drinking the same iced tea and most probably were gonna have the same desert. Segregation, I concluded, was nothing more than geography. Sitting there by myself, I started to chuckle. People sure did get hot and bothered about segregation. Guess there was supposed to be some kind of point to it, but it sure didn't make much sense to me.

As we drove home that night after dinner, Mr. Stewart asked me how I liked the food.

"Good chicken," I said.

"I'm sorry about all that, Willie," he said with an edge of sadness in his voice.

"Don't you worry none," I said, watching him in the rear view mirror. He didn't look so good...that meal hadn't helped him like I'd hoped.

"Does that sort of thing happen to you much?"

"Nah," I drawled...then snorted, "Once, though, in the army a group of us in uniform stopped in a restaurant just outside Richmond, Virginia...there we were...two whites and two blacks."

"Were there other people in the restaurant?"

"About three or four tables full, I think. We ordered four chicken plates then all the fuss started. They refused to serve Charles Cole and me. That was it...all four of us started raising sand, ya know, kicking up a fuss, until they called in the MP's from nearby Fort Lee. But when the MP's showed up, they were split too – one white and one black."

"What did they do?" asked Mr. Stewart, quite interested. "Did they haul you off?"

I smiled. "Hardly, suh."

When Richard Moore, he was the white MP, asked the restaurant owner *why* he wouldn't serve us, he said, "Because them boys are black."

Sergeant Moore studied us up real close like, kinda like in a joking way, looked back at the restaurant owner and announced, "You're exactly right...they *are.*" Then he looked back at us real and asked, "What did you boys order for dinner?"

"Four chicken plates," we answered in chorus.

Moore, cool as a cucumber, looked back at the restaurant owner and said, 'Make that *six* plates. My friend here and I are going to join these fellas for dinner."

Mr. Stewart laughed. "I bet the owner was hopping."

"He sure was," I said. "But not near as mad as when we finished our food."

"Why, what happened *then?*"

"Moore told the owner he shoulda served us to start with instead of calling the MP's who had bigger problems to wrestle with."

"You don't say."

"Know what that white MP said *next?*"

"What?"

"Since you inconvenienced us all," he said real matter-of-fact as he picked his large frame up off his chair, "*We ain't paying.*" Rest of us beat it out of there fast, but not him...no, suh. He took his own sweet time leaving...just moseyed on out of there slow as you please...like he was enjoying a Sunday stroll. Never figured a white MP would end up getting me a free meal in the name of segregation...but that's exactly how it turned out.

Mr. Stewart chuckled. My little story seemed to pick him up a might so I hoped he'd be feeling better the next day.

We got into Pinehurst very late that night, so I was later than usual getting to work the next morning. Mr. Stewart lived just outside the village. I had a key to his house so I opened the door quiet as I could and made my way to the front. I called out to him but he didn't respond. When I reached his bedroom, the door was ajar. I pushed it open real gentle and found Mr. Stewart sitting at his desk. He had a gun in his hand. First I thought he was upset with me for being late and was fixing to shoot me...but he didn't move. His face was white...much whiter than usual...unnatural white. It was only after I saw the trail of blood down the left side of his chin that I realized the poor man had shot himself. I ran to get the police, but they thought I'd killed my boss and I found myself in some serious real trouble. Didn't come easy but I finally was cleared of any wrong doing. After that experience I decided my place was on the Pinehurst links.

Gentle Ben

A little while after I came back to caddying, Julius Boros, who started his career as an accountant for Southern Pines Golf Club, introduced me to Ben Crenshaw. Mr. Crenshaw, then and now, is a real peach of a man...is known as "Gentle Ben" in the golfing world...and for good reason. Ben Crenshaw is wonderful pleasant to be around. He's good to everyone and is comfortable with anyone...knows how to treat a caddie too! Mr. Crenshaw is aces...always starts off with a warm smile that puts a caddie at ease...sets the tone for the round. I never had a problem caddying for him, and I don't know any Pinehurst caddie who has.

"You sure know you're way around these courses," he once told me...coming from a man like him, that comment was the highest of praise. Ben Crenshaw is a true student of the game...always knows what to appreciate about a golf course, especially about the greens. Now he for sure got a gentle nature, but he's still one fierce competitor. Mr. Crenshaw is one of the few pros I know who *enjoys* playing Course Number 3. He likes the challenge of that course's tough greens with elephants buried in them and the downright painful false fronts. I expect he likes Number 3 because he can tame those greens better than anyone...to this day he's the best putter I ever seen.

But Ben Crenshaw knows the history of the game, too...always has had a long fascination about Donald Ross and his prized layout. It's no wonder Robert Dedman, owner of Pinehurst Resort, reached out to Mr. Crenshaw and his partner, Bill Coore, to renovate Number 2. It needed *something*. Mr. Ross had left it in 1948 fulla wire grass and sand, so the two men set to pouring over the Pinehurst archives. They wanted to refashion that Ross dream of having a wee bit of

Scotland in the bosom of the North Carolina Sandhills.

But I remember long before Mr. Coore and him took on the project, Mr. Crenshaw told me, "There's too much green on Number 2. They need to return this course to the way Donald Ross intended."

"How's that?" I asked.

"He had vision, Willie," he said. "He took a piece of ordinary land and carved it into a golf layout masterpiece. Gave the holes the definition they deserve. And the greens...He turned them upside down because he knew how to fit them with traps. He moved only *just the right number of those traps* strategically away from those greens to make them...well, diabolical. Approaching those greens from those traps really tests the best of golfers."

Just goes to show even long before he started wading through the Pinehurst archives trying to piece together a complete picture for Donald Ross's crowning achievement, Mr. Crenshaw already had a vision for it. So I think the Scotsman and him thought the same when it came to this great game.

A Great Announcer and Even Better Player

I caddied for Ben Crenshaw several times in the 1960s. During the Hall of Fame tournaments, he introduced me to Johnny Miller. We were standing on the 1st tee of Number 2 and just the way Mr. Miller introduced himself, I knew right away I was gonna like this man.

"So you think you're a good caddie," he challenged. "When I go out, I want a good caddie."

He never cracked a smile, but I knew he was messing with me.

"You can have the best," I sass mouthed him smiling, "Or you can go back and get the rest."

He broke into a smile of his own, but before he could say another word, Ben Crenshaw closed the conversation. "If you want a good caddie, Willie's the one to get...but not this day." Johnny Miller has this great, wonderful, dry, sense of humor...to this day he loves to needle me. I remember a time during the 2002 U.S. Women's Open at Pine Needles Golf Resort...I was caddying for fourteen-year-old Morgan Pressel. On the 18th hole of the practice round, she parked her approach shot three feet from the pin. Suddenly from the tower to the left of the green rang out a real familiar voice.

"I used to not like that Willie McRae," Johnny called. "But I sure do love him now."

That got both Ms. Pressel and me laughing. Unfortunately Morgan missed the cut that Friday, so I was free the next day. Mr. Miller, Jim Nance and Roger Maltbie all had the afternoon off too so they came to Pinehurst to play Number 2.

Of course, I was on Johnnie's bag. "Now, Mr. McRae, we're going to see just what kind of caddie you are," he challenged.

They played from the tips.

That day Mr. Miller seemed more interested in learning how I happened to caddy for Morgan Pressel in the Women's U.S. Open than he did about playing golf. I spent the first three holes telling him the story and answering questions while he rolled along...birdied each of those holes just as easy as you please.

"You're on fire," I said.

"You keep handing me the right club, Willie," he replied, "and we just might make history today."

Can't remember ever seeing a golfer so relaxed...he was laughing and carrying on with his friends while shooting the round of his life. I remember a newspaper article said I was on his bag when he shot that fabulous 63 in the final round of the 1972 U.S. Open. But that wasn't so...Andy Martinez caddied for him that day. But I do remember that round...seemed like he threw the ball to within ten feet of every hole on Oakmont, hitting every green in regulation. That Saturday afternoon on Number 2 was no different. Just like in '72, he birdied the first four holes...never did show his mortal side until he made routine pars on the next three holes.

"Enough of this, Willie," he joked. "I believe it's time to birdie a few."

I don't think he was joking at all 'cause he rifled off two more birdies on 8 and 9. The 600-yard par 5, 10th brought him back to reality with par, but then he soared back into the birdie zone. For the next six holes he went four under par.

"I'm doing pretty well, aren't I, Willie?" he queried after he drained the putt on 16.

What he was *really* asking me here was if he was close to the course record on Number 2. I didn't want to give him a straight answer 'cause I didn't want to jinx him. He'd actually missed a few "makeable" putts along the way, but even so I thought the 62 course record was within his reach. "You own the course today," was all I said.

He seemed to concentrate more on the 17th, but left it with a par. The banter with his friends continued as the foursome strolled to the 18th tee. The way he was striking the ball, I felt confident he could birdie the last. I felt even better when he ran his approach shot to within five feet of the hole. I gave him a read...the green had less break than it looked. He'd been putting real fine all day, back low and through with confidence, but now three inches back on his back swing, I shut my eyes. It was the first time that day he lifted the blade. When a golfer does that he'll either push or pull the putt. *Johnny Miller pulled it.* The ball settled an inch left of the hole and a stroke from the course record. Though unofficial, he tied Hale Irwin's course record of 62, the year Hale won Hall of Fame Tournament.

Sadly that Saturday wasn't the only day Johnny Miller's magic putting stroke failed. It started giving him trouble pretty regular. But I'll tell you if it'd stayed with him, Johnny Miller would still be winning golf tournaments and doing a lot less announcing.

Mr. Generosity

Now my brother, Ted, worked for Harvie Ward, the head professional at nearby Foxfire Golf and Country Club. Like his contemporary, Arnold Palmer, this man knew how to treat people and they loved him for it. Might say he was an institution in the Pinehurst area...his picture still hangs in the clubhouse hallway.

I caddied for him several times and was devastated when he passed on well before his time. You've heard about someone who'd give you "the shirt off his back?" Well that was this gentleman. Whenever times got tough, he always wanted to help.

"Mr. Generosity" — Harvie Ward

"I don't care what you need the money for, Willie," he'd say. "Just *take* it."

It bothered me accepting money from the man, but I knew he'd be offended if I refused.

"Listen, Willie, I started poor and there's no blame in that," he told me.

"I come *up* poor," I responded, "and I'm *still* poor."

He chuckled at that and wrapped his arm around my shoulder. "You'll get 'unpoor' like me," Harvie Ward affirmed. "Just give it time."

The sincerity in his tone made me believe what he said...but I'm still waiting.

The Integration of Church and Golf
Chi Chi Rodriquez

I'm a part time preacher and occasionally give sermons at the church in Taylortown. Over the years religion's helped me out of many jams, and I've tried to push my kids and grandkids in its direction much as possible. I grew up settling scores with my fists. But now religion gives me an anchor and allows me to handle minor intolerances. I've never tried to preach religion while caddying, but once when toting bags for a couple of players, the exchange of faith came natural and easy.

Chi Chi Rodriquez is a true religious man, and he once said, no matter what he's doing, "I can feel the Church in the background." He told me religion was good for golf and made the players better role models for kids.

"Golf is rather unique that way," he told me. "Like with other sports, Willie, they're a lot of people looking at you, waiting for you to perform, but in baseball or football you're part of a *team*. In golf you're all alone. You need to say that prayer or two especially when things go wrong.

"Willie, I believe God was ready to wipe man off the face of the earth," he once told me. "*Why?* Because man just was too human and couldn't live up to his Creator's expectations...but he gave him one more chance and sent his Son to save the world. Do you believe that, Willie?"

"I surely do."

After that Mr. Rodriquez and me had many candid conversations that I truly believe helped my soul. It was easy to talk to the man since we shared both religion and golf as common bonds.

"I remember this tournament in Maryland," he said. "We came to this par 5...bit of a dogleg right with a sizable creek running in front of the green. I drove my drive big, but to the right and into some pretty ugly rough. Because of the deep rough, it was not only hard to find the ball, but to identify it. Well, within the five minutes allotted time, we found one."

"Was it yours?"

"I hit it about thirty feet but when we located it again, we discovered it wasn't my ball. Then we came across another ball. I hit it with the same result, but again it wasn't mine. The crowd grew edgy as the next group stood waiting on the tee."

"What did you do?"

"Willie, I prayed hard that I would find my ball. Lo and behold we found another one. When I hit it, it shot out of that rough like it was on a mission, soaring high and landing soft just before the creek, at a perfect angle to the pin."

"Was it *your* ball?"

"I declared it so to the entire crowd right after I hit it...was still in the air," Chi Chi said, smiling broadly. "Faith, Willie, *faith*. I believed it to be so and it *was*."

"What did you end up getting on the hole?" I asked.

He winked, "Routine birdie."

Tom Lehman

Tom Lehman is also a religious man, but real different in personality from Mr. Rodriquez. A soft-spoken gentleman, Mr. Lehman is one of the most considerate golfers I've had the pleasure of caddying for. I once caddied for him in a sponsor event...that's where a golfer will play a few holes with his sponsors...I guess for marketing purposes. He only played about a dozen holes or so that day and was easy to club for. I liked the way he struck the ball. Never heard him utter a negative word neither...he was always positive. He thanked me for giving him the right clubs and praised how I read the greens. The way he spoke I knew he had a "deep soul" and a calming effect on those around him. Not loud or boisterous, he was simply a joy to be with.

On the 11th hole, after his shot didn't go the way he woulda liked, he said something that put me in mind of the great Bobby Jones, "You read it right, Willie. I just didn't."

Now a man like that you wouldn't figure to fail to tip his caddie, but that's exactly what he did...when the dust settled, he just left with his small entourage without offering me *anything* extra for my efforts. Sure...I got the standard caddie fee, but I just thought a man like Tom Lehman woulda tipped me some. Thought about it for a week or so...then let it go.

But Tom Lehman thought about it for a whole year.

When he returned a year later, he sought me out and apologized profusely. "Gee, Willie," he said as he handed me a hundred dollars, "Last year in all the fuss, I forgot to tip you and that wasn't right."

I smiled. "Not a problem."

"I hope you won't charge me interest," he kidded. "Seriously, please forgive me."

A man like that never should have to beg forgiveness. I only tell the story now to show why not.

Great Smile, Great Man, Great Golfer

Occasionally a pro golfer will visit Pinehurst with his sponsors. They most often like to play courses 5 and 4 'cause those are where players normally qualify for tournaments. When Peter Jacobsen came to town, it was no different.

"Willie," he said up front. "Tell me the trouble shots and where to hit the ball."

Mr. Jacobsen flashed me that warm smile of his and I knew right off that this was gonna be a fun day. For the first couple of holes, I took the driver out of his hands. Then on the par 5 3rd hole, after he clobbered his driver down the center of the fairway, I handed him a 5-iron.

"I can't get there from here," he said. "The pin's back and it's uphill."

"Trust me, you can," I said.

"I don't believe so."

"Trust me," I told him. "I been clubbing people for a long time and I know how this course behaves much better than you."

"How long have you been here?"

"Since 1943."

Peter Jacobsen straightened but still wasn't convinced. "Willie, you haven't seen me hit enough shots," he insisted. "Give me the 4."

I didn't move or say a thing, just stood there holding out the 5.

He was real reluctant about taking it...but he finally did. I could tell he still wasn't convinced. But he pinched the turf perfectly with that 5-iron and the ball soared high and straight, landing three feet from the stick...*an eagle.*

He shook his head in disbelief at his own triumph. "I never thought I'd make it."

I smiled thinking that would be the end of it. But through the whole round I had to keep denying Peter Jacobsen his driver and giving him less club than he thought he needed. On the 8th hole he hit the driver wedge to a foot below the pin.

"Damn," exclaimed one of his sponsors. "You need to hire Willie full time."

Mr. Jacobsen chuckled. "I couldn't do that to Pinehurst. This is where he belongs."

We were having a good ol' time. By the back 9, the players and caddies were bantering back and forth pretty good. On the par 5, 14th, I let Mr. Jacobsen pound the driver, which he did long and strong. He ended up with a side hill lie to an elevated green. He would have to choke up on the club. He looked at me expectantly, but didn't say a word.

"You've got a 3-wood, a 4-wood and a 5-wood," I said. "A 3's too much and 4's questionable...take the 5-wood and leave none of it back here."

He did just that and managed to get a towering draw to just ten feet from the flag. When he shook his head in disbelief, I smiled and thought sure after this last shot Peter Jacobsen would never question me again. But he did. After he lipped out his eagle putt, we moved our way to the famous Cathedral Hole. I felt confident as I handed him an 8-iron.

He laughed, *"No way."*

I cocked my head, the 8-iron extended in my hand.

"Willie, I just don't think..."

"That's right," I said. *"Don't think*...and don't mess up and make a liar out of me, neither."

His friends and him laughed. Some might worry I coulda jinxed him with that command, but I knew Peter Jacobsen wouldn't let me down. Sure enough he came through. The ball soared high in the air. It was one of those shots where everyone watching knew the ball had a chance of going in the hole. Gave it one good try too, but then it one-hopped before cozying up ten inches from the cup.

Mr. Jacobsen shot 67 that day, good enough to qualify for *any* tournament.

Now he certainly didn't have to, but after the round he told me, "No caddie's ever clubbed me better. Thanks Willie."

I appreciated that generous compliment. "Some guys come out and just tote the bag," I replied. "I prefer to caddy."

The King Goes Under the Ropes

Fans rightly put Arnold Palmer up on a pedestal. That pedestal just keeps getting higher every time he shows us his humble humanity...hitching up his pants, "curlicuing" the club at the end of his swing, and flashing that slightly off-center smile have all endeared us to the man. Mr. Palmer became the *King* because he's *Everyman*...the person everyone would like to be.

Although he's won over sixty tournaments, his golf swing will never make a golf instruction book. His back swing is a little too quick and his kind of jerky follow though lacks an Ernie El's easy finish. But the six inches before and after the ball, are dead on perfect. His hands always come through the ball the same way and at impact the club head is where it needs to be.

Early in his career he'd come down to Pinehurst from his alma mater, Wake Forest University in North Carolina. I knew the first time I caddied for him he was gonna be a star...and I told him so. "You're gonna be a great golfer someday," I proclaimed.

"I'm trying, Willie," he said, flashing me his signature smile.

A golf course is just a different place altogether when he's on it. The character of the man rubs off on the course, enhancing it that much more. Back in his earlier days...I think during a Hall of Fame Tournament...Mr. Palmer actually went under the ropes to sign autographs for a group of kids. It was a practice round so no one seemed bothered by it. But the next day during the tournament, he did the same thing again on the par 5, 16th hole. When an official approached to tell him he was in danger of slow play, he responded, "We make our money here with the fans. A minute or so to say thanks won't hurt."

Arnold Palmer has always respected the galleries and other golfers more than any other player out there.

In another Hall of Fame Tournament "Arnie's Army" swelled early on...just like it always did. He'd just hit a magnificent approach shot

Arnold Palmer (L) and Harvie Ward (R)

some five feet from the hole. The crowd immediately pressed onward, but the King called out to halt its progress. Now his playing partners that day were Julius Boros and Charlie Sifford who was one of the first touring black golfers. Both men had out-driven the man who was controlling the crowd lining the fairway.

"Please wait until Mr. Sifford shoots," Mr. Palmer requested...his army of fans immediately froze in place. "Charlie's a golfer just like me. And so too is Mr. Boros. Clap for them as you would for me, or please, don't clap at all. Thank you."

No, Mr. Palmer, thank *you*.

Pot Bunkers – infamous in number on course Number 4

CHAPTER TEN

THE PINEHURST TOURNAMENTS

"*I*s Arnold Palmer really that great a guy?" asks paisley tie.

"*Oh, he had an eye for the women," I say. "And believe you me, they had an eye for him too...but there's never been a better man for the game."*

"*So what about the new guys like Tiger Woods or Rory McElroy?" pipes up the fella wearing a red and black tie.*

"*Been on the course with Tiger, but I never caddied for him," I reply. "His childhood coach once told me he always knew that boy was special...said when the other kids were messing around at practice, Tiger would be off to the side doing jumping jacks. That kid was focused. Still is. He's my bet to get twenty majors."*

"*Tell us about some of the tournaments you've caddied in," yellow tie asks. "Like the North South Amateur."*

"*That was a pro event some years back, wasn't it?" a newcomer adds.*

"*Sure was," I tell them, until Sammy Snead and Tommy Bolt got into it a few times."*

My tidbit brought a chorus of, "Oh, I want to hear about that."

"Ah, the North South," I muse, "So many fond memories... and **crazy** moments. Like the time Billy Joe Patton — now there was a truly remarkable amateur — was coming up on the 20th hole of his match."

"What happened?" pursues one of the newcomers.

"His opponent...can't just catch his name right now...and him were at the 2nd hole on Number 2 of a sudden death playoff. Now there's a road called Midland Road that flanks that hole on the left. Well Billy Joe had hooked his drive real bad like and landed in a tough spot up close to the road. So he's standing there trying to figure out what to do when this woman pulls up in a car and rolls down the window. 'Do you know where I can find a room in this town?' she asks Billy Joe.

"You're kidding," howls paisley tie.

"For real?" gasps someone from the back.

"What did he do?" asks another newcomer slack-jawed in surprise.

"Damnedest thing," I recall. "He looked up at her like answering her question was the only thing on his mind. 'If I lose this hole,' he said. 'You can have mine.' "

A chorus of "no's" follows.

"And you know what she did?" I go on. "She turned that car right around, pulled off Midland and parked just back of the green. Of course, Billy Joe had to chop out of where he was and it didn't go so good for him. He ended up having to concede the hole and the round. When he did that, there she was, ready and willing to take his room key."

"Who was she, what was her name?" someone calls from the back.

"Haven't a clue," I reply. "Don't think Mr. Patton ever knew neither. He just collected his things and she moved in later. Can you imagine something like that ever happening today?"

A number of men shake their heads...one of them snorts, "Are you kidding? Today she wouldn't even be allowed to drive down that road during tournament play."

Now when Diamondhead took over Pinehurst in 1970, William H. Maurer stepped up to the helm. He had big ideas for the *new* village but met with a lot of resistance from the townspeople 'cause they thought things were just fine like they were. Mr. Maurer paid no mind to all the fuss...he plowed right ahead anyway and spent a ton of money converting the hotels and storefronts into a town that he proclaimed would attract a new generation of leisure seekers. He had nine thousand acres to fool with and he was determined to develop every last square inch.

Diamondhead initiated the World Golf Hall of Fame back in 1974 and President Gerald Ford came down, along with a bunch of dignitaries and professional golfers, for the induction of Bobby Jones and Walter Hagen. Then from 1973 to 1983 Pinehurst hosted an annual PGA Golf tournament. First they called the event the World Open. Then Colgate became a sponsor for a few years...anyway the tournament finally ended up wearing the banner of the Hall of Fame Classic.

But Diamondhead's plans didn't pan out exactly like they were intended. By the late '70s, a thousand lots still hadn't sold and while those early tournaments drew up to 240 players, the eight rounds of grueling golf failed to attract the big guns, like Jack Nicklaus and Johnny Miller. By 1976, Mr. Maurer realized he'd underestimated the magnetism of the traditional Pinehurst charm so he tried to reign in his real estate recklessness. But so much development already had gone on. The residents, all up in arms, complained that the pristine courses of old with their magnificent views were being penned in by too many houses and condos...got to be worse than a soap opera. All this fussing caused more than half the land Diamondhead originally planned to develop to remain untouched.

So with all this mess playing out behind me, I kept on caddying...caddied in most of those tournaments, too. Found myself on the bag of Stewart Taylor in the Pro-Am Events. He was a southerner coming from South Carolina – first arrived in Pinehurst as a junior golfer. Now I know he came to the Pro-Am with high hopes of bringing Number 2 to its knees but those greens, like bowls turned upside down, turned the tables on him pretty bad.

He shot 86 back then, but moved his game up considerable in the 1979 Hall of Fame Classic. That event teamed three amateurs with a professional. They set it up so the winner would walk away with $5,000, plus a $60,000 golf course lot in nearby Pinewild. Second place would only garner a measly $3,000. They played the two-day event on courses Number 2 and 7. Mr. Taylor and Bobby Groff tied with rounds of 67 and 71...so they came to Number 2 to play a sudden death playoff. On the 2nd hole Stewart airmailed the green and his chances of winning started looking right grim. Now he pitched back real nice to within six feet, but Mr. Groff had a par putt *half* that length. Always the competitor, Mr. Stewart drained his putt, but poor Mr. Bobby somehow managed to leave his short. *The tournament belonged to Stewart Taylor.* So he won the money and the lot. I heard he later ended up selling that lot...used the money to send his son, Elliott, to North Carolina State University... right smart man that Mr. Stewart.

Temper Can Ruin a Golf Match,
If Not an Entire Tournament

One of the main reasons Pinehurst has enjoyed its reputation through the years is 'cause of the number of golf tournaments that been held there. Right from the days of the resort's founder, James Tufts, Pinehurst hosted tournaments marking any and all occasions...they all flourished, too. The North South Tournament started as a women's event way back in 1903, but later expanded to include both men and women amateurs...even became one of the most celebrated PGA events...well, up until 1951 that is. I think the tournament in large part dropped its professional series after that year 'cause Sam Snead and Tommy Bolt just didn't get along.

I was just a teenager in 1949 when I drew the fiery Tommy Bolt for the tournament. He was on his "A" game that week but I never met a man whose name suited his personality better. Years later he was featured in the sports section of most major newspapers for hurling his golf clubs — bag and all — into a lake. Tommy Bolt was a fine golfer, but he was more than just a tad excitable.

As luck would have it Tommy Bolt and Mr. Snead were paired in the third round. I was on Tommy Bolt's bag while Jimmy Steed

Tommy Bolt

Sam Snead

carried "Slammin' Sammy's." Mr. Snead already had won the North South Tournament three times and had finished second another three times. He owned this event largely 'cause of his caddie. *Lord, did Jimmy know how to club Sam Snead*...Jimmy Steed caddied for Mr. Snead in the Greensboro Open, too...and Mr. Snead won *that* North Carolina tournament *eight* times. There's some who say that if Jimmy had been on Sam Snead's bag for all his tournaments, he probably woulda won well over 100 events. "Sam had a great many talents, but selecting clubs wasn't one of them," claimed Bill Campbell, a fellow competitor at the time. "Jimmy had a knack of giving Sam the right clubs."

Now being paired with Sam Snead mighta intimidated most players but it just rankled Tommy Bolt. On the 11th hole of Number 2 that day, Mr. Bolt held a three-shot lead. He'd left his 8-iron approach less than a foot from the hole. In my excitement I hurried on ahead of the golfers, wondering how much I'd make caddying for the tournament winner. I figured Mr. Snead would reach the green with a sour look on his face, but when I set down the bag and turned to the golfers, I saw it was the other way around. Tommy Bolt was fit to be tied. I darted a glance at Jimmy, but he only shrugged.

Mr. Snead sure knew how to rile that hot-tempered Mr. Bolt...and that's precisely what he did this time around.

"I'm not going to play with you anymore," Tommy complained. " 'Cause I can buy you...you and your stinking Montgomery Ward pants!"

Jimmy and me stood rooted in shock...you coulda heard a pin

drop throughout the gallery.

Mr. Bolt whipped around to me. *"Get that ball!"* he barked.

"Ya mean pick it up?" I stammered in disbelief.

"I mean exactly that," he barked. "You get paid by the week so what are you worried about?"

"You sure you wanna – " I stopped in mid-sentence 'cause I could see fumes pouring out the man's ears. He was *dead* serious. And you coulda heard another pin drop as I approached the green to retrieve his ball. Then I walked back and picked up his golf bag without a word. To my surprise, the gallery actually applauded as we trudged back to the clubhouse. Guess they musta respected the tongue-lashing Mr. Bolt put on Slammin' Sammy. Back at the clubhouse Tommy stuffed my hand with a wad of greenbacks, then marched over to the scoreboard and withdrew. "I just won't play with Sam Snead again," he gave as his only excuse for disrupting and withdrawing from a tournament he woulda led by four strokes.

Not to be outdone, Sam Snead picked up the following year and stomped off the course for reasons I'll never know. He was done with the North South...didn't even bother coming in 1951. With Mr. Snead out, Tommy Bolt returned and won that tournament in its final PGA year.

Practice Makes Nearly Perfect

In May of 1970, a five-handicapper came to play in the North South Amateur and I was lucky enough to caddy for him. A lawyer from Fayetteville, Mike Williford was a great guy. His burly size really let him boom the ball and gave him huge potential for the game.

But watching him on the range, I could see he needed a little help. After a few holes, I saw three things he needed to cure before he'd be tournament competitive. Mike got short and quick on the course. He bent his elbow some on his back swing and his quickness made him look up too soon on his follow through. That unfortunate combination made him suffer from the dreaded over-the-top move.

He listened to what I had to say...then being a glutton for punishment he came back for more. He visited Pinehurst often that summer and we worked together on both the range and the course. By October, Mike was a scratch player and ready for tournament golf. The next year he qualified for the match play event.

His first match was against Bill Harvey. Both men played steady golf for eight holes...even par. But on the 9th my man broke through with a birdie. When he took the ball from the cup, his face was wearing the expression I'd waited near a year to see...he beamed with confidence, well-earned from a year of hard work. Birdies on the following hole and on 13 brought us to the 15th three-up.

Months earlier, I never I woulda been saying to him, "Might as well knock him off here and get ready for the next match." But that's exactly what I found myself doing now.

Mike looked at me and winked. "Let's do it."

Sure enough we did...with a birdie 2...so after shaking hands all around, we headed for the clubhouse, winners 4 and 3.

In the round of 32, our match with Downing Gray played out like a game of ping pong. Mike won the 2nd hole, lost the next, picked up the 5th, but dropped the 9th. Stepping onto the 18th tee, we stayed all tied. Mike hadn't lost the confidence he had the day before...no suh! He just knew he was in a dogfight and wasn't quite sure how to handle this mongrel.

"You don't want to take this guy extra holes," I said.

"I sure don't," Mike replied.

"Believe you me, he's thinking the same way," I continued. "So let's end this thing *now*."

On that hole, Mike came of age as a golfer and a competitor. He had the tools, but this was no Sunday morning round. He dug deep, committed to his drive and parked it smack in the middle of the fairway. With the match on the line, he trusted his own abilities on his 7-iron approach shot. There was no bent elbow on the back swing, and no coming out of the swing too soon...he was just as smooth as silk from start to finish. Mike had arrived...knew it soon as that ball sailed high and straight for the pin. He drained the five-foot putt and we walked off the green 1-up.

I know Mike reaching the sweet 16 surprised a lot of people...maybe even me a little. But after watching him handle that 155-yard approach shot on 18, I knew he could do it. If he was gonna lose that week, someone would have to flat out beat him.

His next opponent was an incredible golfer. Partially blind, the player, whose name escapes me now, showed everyone real quick that he belonged. Even with his handicap, the man was a real ball striker. Now Mike continued his strong play, but even so, the two men were tied after 9.

"What do I have to do to beat this guy?" Mike asked in frustration.

"Throw birdies at him," I replied.

I said it kinda joking, but as things turned out that's exactly what it took. Mike birdied 10 and 14 then came to the 16th tee with a two-shot lead.

"He's parring everything in sight," Mike said.

"Then birdie this hole," I countered. "It's a par 5. You're longer than he is. What's the problem?"

There was none. Mike lofted a 5-wood dead on the hole, two-putted and took the match, 3 and 2. He'd made it to the elite eight.

Mike ended up losing at that level, 4 and 3...didn't hit the ball solid like he'd been doing. His rival, George Parlor, fired five under. In a letter he sent me a few years later, Mike claimed, "I never seriously challenged for the title." But he was wrong...his putter just failed him that round, that's all. I'll never forget him thanking me for my help. He wrote, "Willie, you can read those greens from the highway." Generous with his praise, that man was...

And he was much too humble in that letter. Mike had gained the tools to win — had the swing, the attitude, the confidence. To this day he probably still doesn't know how good he was, but he sure was just that. They say golf is a game of inches. Some days the putts fall; others they don't. In just one short year, Mike became one quality player...any one of those final eight competitors coulda won that year...him as much as anyone else. I hope by telling his story here, he'll finally appreciate how good a player and know how competitive he was.

The Two U.S. Opens

In 1970, I caddied for a fine man, the gracious winner of the North South Amateur, Gary Cowan. That tournament was one incredible display of golf...still can see each shot...each putt so vivid in my mind. That man was on fire that week in May, throwing darts at each pin...was like them balls had radar on them. Gary went well under par each day, winning by margins anywhere from 3 and 2 to a final 5 and 4 in the 36-hole championship round. Gary was way good enough to turn pro...guess he never did because of his thriving insurance business.

Many people have asked me how I did in the two U.S. Opens held at Pinehurst. Payne Stewart had wowed the crowd in the 1999 U.S. Open by sinking that famous twenty-footer on the 72nd hole. 1999...that was the year I had been Number 1 in line to get a bag in the first Open at Pinehurst...but I ended up having to decline.

That Monday I was still waiting to hear whose bag it would be, and was whiling away the time painting a man's house with my son, Gordon. We were busy working when I heard an anxious voice call out, "Gordon, where's your daddy at?"

Knew right off something was wrong.

Roland, another one of my sons, had been in a car accident. Roland had been driving. There was one car ahead of him on his side of the road and a truck coming toward them down the opposite lane. The truck driver musta dropped a piece of paper or something on the floor of his cab. Well he bent down to get whatever it was and lost control of his truck. The car ahead of Roland swerved into a ditch. But my Roland wasn't so fortunate...he didn't find the ditch...he ended up going head on into the truck that had veered onto his side of the road.

I remember that drive to the Fayetteville hospital...just sat staring aimless out the car window...all empty and blank. Felt like someone had just come up and kicked me in the stomach for no good reason...couldn't rightly get my mind around what had happened... couldn't believe it was true...didn't want to. The sky looked like lead...flat, dull and gray. Been driving along for a while when a patch of gray opened up to let the sun peek through...was like its own little miracle. But that moment of light was brief, so very brief. The sky soon closed up gray again...too soon...just way too soon...and I knew...*Jacob's Ladder*...I turned to Gordon who was driving and said, "Our Roland's gone."

Found out later, he passed right about then. Both of his sons were in the car with him that day, but somehow survived that wreck ...thank you, Lord. Today they're fine young men.

In 2005 I drew David Oh, a young pro from California. A couple years earlier I'd been inducted into the World Golf Hall of Fame so I'd already gained a bit of notoriety of my own. The crowds lining the fairways were pretty thick that year. They were anticipating a dramatic repeat of Payne Stewart's magical comeback. As we ambled down the 14th hole of Number 2, a few in the crowd called, "There goes Willie McRae. Hey Willie!"

"Why are they cheering for you?" David asked, amazed. "I'm the player."

I smiled, showing all my teeth. "That might be...but *I'm* the celebrity."

Mr. Oh laughed and while he missed the cut that year, we had a great time. The media actually wanted to interview me after each day — for local color, so to speak, or to highlight the history of

Pinehurst. They took pictures of me, my grandson, Darick, and his son. Some say I had more press time than the champion, Michael Campbell. But during my fifteen minutes-of-fame, I managed to get David Oh an interview too. I slipped away while he was telling the interviewer how proud he was to be in his first U.S. Open. I didn't want to disturb the player's moment in the sun.

Boy, How the Young Can Play

In my later years, I had the great pleasure to caddie for two future superstars, Morgan Pressell, in the 2003 North South Amateur, and Peter Uihlein, in the 2008 U.S. Amateur.

Now just like I told you before, I caddied for Ms. Pressell a year earlier in the Women's U.S. Open at Pine Needles Golf Resort. After she qualified at the tender age of 14, her grandfather called the caddie master, Jimmy Smith, and asked him to recommend a caddie for the tournament. Jimmy gave the man my name. Now Morgan had a beautiful swing and was a whale-full of talent, but didn't quite have the maturity...kinda wore her heart on her sleeve. Morgan ended up not making the cut at the Open, and took that disappointment real hard.

After having a good cry, she thanked me for my help.

"You're gonna be a fine golfer," I told her. "And I should know 'cause I been with most of the finest golfers of the past sixty years."

That brought a small chuckle and stopped some of the tears. "I'm thinking of coming to Pinehurst in two years to play in the North South," she confided.

"Oh, that's a good idea," I said. "You'll be ready then."

True to her promise she visited me again two years later. Her grandfather sought out the caddie master and asked if I was still around.

"Is a five-pound robin fat?" chided Jimmy Smith.

"Good," the man replied. "Willie can do more for her than I can."

At sixteen, believe me, she was ready. She gained the field of 64 while making it look no more than a graceful Sunday afternoon stroll. She won her first match hands down, 6 and 5. Morgan continued to cruise the next day with a 5 and 4 victory in the morning, then another 6 and 5 win in the afternoon...didn't falter in the Elite Eight and semi-finals neither. She won handily 4 and 3, then 5 and 4. But still, I started to worry...I knew she hadn't met her match yet. If she did in the finals, would she have the maturity to hang tough and go the distance?

But in the finals she showed no signs of letting up. She birdied the first three holes and came to the 4th tee 2-up. After a big drive down the middle of the fairway, I handed her a 3-wood for her second shot to the par 5.

"I can't hit a 3-wood that far," she said. "I think I'll lay up."

"Now I thought you said at the start you were gonna to listen to me," I scolded her. "The wind will help you here. Just trust your swing."

Without uttering a word, she took the club, looked at the shot from behind, planted herself and sailed the ball dead at the hole...three-feet, eagle.

She went easy on her opponent for the next several holes. Birdies on 17 and 18 let her enjoy her lunch with a 5-up lead...was a much different day from the disappointment of two years ago. That entire experience with Morgan was a joy. After every good shot, I'd pat her on the shoulder and she'd laugh. Really wanted to tell her something, but I didn't want to jinx her. Never woulda been able to forgive myself if I did that. Keep her loose, I told myself...just keep her loose.

On the difficult 2nd hole of the afternoon round, she went 6-up. Still I wouldn't tell her. Then on the 4th hole, the one she eagled in the morning, she reached the green in two and poured in a birdie for 7-up. Still I didn't say a word. Up until then she'd been all business. I'd never seen a girl her age hit the ball so far. But on the next hole, when her 5-wood reached the hardest hole on the golf course, she couldn't keep it in no more. She turned to me and even before she gave me that big hug, I could see it in her eyes. Confidence had replaced those tears from before...she knew she was on her way...she could taste victory.

Wasn't until the 9th hole that her armor started to crack. Morgan had built a 9-up lead. We were standing on the 9th tee when I said, "Win this and we can go home."

But she lost that hole along with the long par 5, 10th where she three-putted. As we came from the green, I watched her confidence slip. There was a new set of tears welling up in her eyes.

"Don't you cry," I scolder her. "You keep focused, ya hear?"

She nodded, raised her head proudly, and we made our way to the 11th tee. "I thought that last putt broke more than you said," she admitted.

Again I couldn't help but think of Bobby Jones. He woulda seen the promise in this young lady and how I wished she coulda known him. "Bobby Jones told me that once, too," I told her.

She caught the importance of the moment. *"He did?"* she said, looking square in my eyes.

"Sure did...same kind of situation, too." It was time to tell her. "If you just halve the next two holes, you'll be the youngest player in history to win this tournament," I said. "And once you do that, think how good you gonna feel."

Sunshine returned to her face. She halved the next two holes and hugged me tight.

"Be sure when you turn pro," I told her when we parted, after our triumphant walk back to the club house, "you get yourself a good caddie."

The next year she returned to defend her title, but lost a painful decision in the final on the 39th hole. Her opponent flew the green, but had a good approach and drained an eight-foot putt. Morgan left her six-footer the smallest suggestion of an inch short, but it was her three putts on the 11th hole sealed her fate that day.

"You got nothing to be ashamed of," I told her as she battled back the tears.

And she didn't...she'd lost on the 39th hole to the world's current Number 1 female golfer. This woman had won five Majors by the time she was twenty-three, and that record remains unmatched by anyone, man or woman. Part of the Asian invasion, her name is Yani Tseng.

What a Difference a Shot Makes

How many times has a golfer looked back over a round only to recognize the one bad shot that really cost him? I'm sure it's happened to everyone who's ever lost a tournament or match.

I'd caddied for Mr. Uihlein once or twice so when his son, Peter, qualified for the 2008 U.S. Amateur in Pinehurst, I was happy to take the bag of the 19-year old college freshman. "I'll do it," I told his father.

I liked Peter Uihlein right from the start. He was a splendid young man, had a get-along-with-everyone personality and maturity far beyond his years. That year he qualified on Number 2 and Number 4. The Bermuda rough there was a straight up six inches tall...to find a ball in *that* rough you had to be looking right down at it...took a lot of strength and flexibility to blast your way out of *that* stuff. So when Peter ripped the ball from the thick rough some one hundred eighty yards to within seven feet of the pin in the qualifying round, I knew I had myself a winner.

He qualified with a 72 and found himself seeded in the middle of the pack. The placement didn't seem to bother him none. He cruised through his first two matches, 6 and 5, then 5 and 3. Peter's game was *perfect* – no mistakes – was almost like he wasn't one of us mere mortals. We entered that fourth round brimming with confidence... but that's where Peter proved human. For the life of me, I can't remember the name of his opponent in that round...but no matter...this match was all about young Uihlein as I see it. He clawed his way through fifteen holes and stood on the 16th tee with a 1-up lead. Though new to the college circuit, Peter had found his first few matches a bit too easy. By this round I could see the pressure mount on him. He'd never been in a spot like this before. Any real golfer has to feel it sooner or later...and it's not so much how they face it that first time that's important...it's what they take away from the experience that matters. The faint-hearted will fold and never will learn to compete...but the strong will take in and store what they learn so they can overcome the next time around.

On the lengthy par 5 16th hole, Peter's nervousness started showing up in his grip. His left hand never seemed settled on the club. This problem tightened his back swing. I could tell right away from the quickness at the top of his swing where his ball was going. He sure had the power and length he needed, but that pull-hook doomed his drive. His ball landed tight to the left and his only shot was up the fairway of the par-3, 17th. Peter hit a 5-wood up near the white tees of that hole which actually put him in a good place to chip it close.

"Forget that drive," I said.

"Already did," he replied.

"Your second shot was perfect," I said as I set the bag down. We looked across at the green where his opponent was waiting, lying two. "Now just chip it on the green and let it roll out to the hole."

Unfortunately he nipped the ball a little too good, so when the ball landed on the green, it checked up eight feet from the pin. After a brilliant first putt, his opponent tapped in for birdie. If Peter could drain his putt, the save would bolster his confidence for the rest of the tournament...probably even for years to come. He read the putt right, but put a little too much juice on it...caused it to skirt to the left side of the hole. We were all square going into 18.

Times like this, a good caddie's worth his weight in gold 'cause he knows just the right thing to encourage his player and steady him up. I looked at my young golfer and directed, "Peter, you can win the entire thing if you just get past this guy. Now do it."

His drive was perfect...so was his 6-iron approach, leaving him five feet from the hole to his rival's 15. I winked at Peter when the other competitor missed his putt. "Left edge. Don't give up the hole," I instructed as I moved away from him.

But Peter hadn't put that drive on the 16th behind him quite yet. I saw the thought of it haunt him as his fingers started to twitch on his putter again. He missed the five-footer and lost on the 19th hole. Still plagued by the hooked drive, he pushed his easy 9-iron approach to the right, then had to stand there and watch helpless as it trickled off the false front of the Donald Ross green.

Did that young man learn from his errant drive? You betcha. He mighta struggled a bit with his game through his freshman year of college, but he came back strong. One year later Peter Uihlein went undefeated in his Walker Cup matches and ended up leading the U.S. team to victory. A year later Peter whooped them all in the U.S. Amateur Championship and became the "Number 1-ranked amateur golfer in the world." And now he has become one of the top professionals on the European Tour.

Took a while...but like all great players, he finally put that bad drive to rest.

Maniac Hill — built in 1913 this famous driving range
has hosted many of golf's greats.
It was here Willie shagged balls for Fred Daly
at the 1951 Ryder Cup,
as well as for Bobby Jones and countless others.

CHAPTER ELEVEN

MY DAYS GOLFING

R ed tie in the pinstripe suit shakes his head. "No wonder Pinehurst has you doing these PR gigs for them," he said. "You've got a hundred stories to share."

I nod and wish I had a glass of water, too...been doing too much talking.

"Tell me," paisley tie joins in, "Who haven't you caddied for?"

"Tiger, for one," I say. "But I been on the course with him."

"What's he like?" asks someone whose tie I can't make out.

"Serious," I reply. "No...focused might be a better way of putting it. Now he's serious 'cause he's thinking. Most golfer's think too much on the course, but with Tiger, it's his way of staying in the game."

They throw out a bunch of golfer names new and old — Jack Nicklaus, Phil Mickelson, Freddy Couples, and Hale Irwin, holder of the official record of 62 on Number 2. I been on the course with most of them, but wasn't on their bags when they played here. My memories of great golfers are much more vivid if I caddied for them.

"Say, Willie," another chimes in. "You've told us about so many of the good times you've had caddying. Isn't there a player or two who you didn't like or maybe, didn't like you?"

I throw back my head and hoot. "Oh, yes...one in particular."

There's new excitement in the crowd. "Tell us," urges yellow tie.

"His name was 'Beebop,' " I recall, "or least that's what every-one called him...used to play in a pretty polished group, too, with the likes of Bob Stranahan and Tommy Armour. That was back in the late '50s...maybe...early '60s. Anyway, this one day I was caddying for Stranahan and Beebop. They were playing their usual Nassau. My two guys were down on the front, but doing a good job on the back."

"How much were they playing for?" someone asks.

I shrug. "Dunno...but not too much. Not like the Money Game. Anyway we come to the 16th green and Beepbop lines up his putt. He had it wrong, but we weren't getting on so good that day so I kept my mouth shut. He pulls up on the putt and says, 'McRae, how many times do I have to tell you? MOVE BACK. I can see your feet!' The pin was tight on the right side of the green, and dangerous close to a big yawning trap."

"What did you do?" asks paisley tie.

"I moved back. I was sure he couldn't see my feet no more, but he comes out of his set-up and barks same thing again, 'McRae, move back.' So I did. 'More,' he hollers. Now I'm already off the green, but I still back up more. Suddenly I lose my footing. wham...fell right into the trap."

They laugh. "What happened then?" someone blurts.

"Lying flat on my back, I yell, 'Can't see my feet now, can ya?' "
They laugh again. "What did Beebop do?"

"Oh, was he pissed," I tell them. "After the round he stormed
into the caddie master's office and let out on me, hollering, 'I don't
want that caddie anymore.' "

"What did the caddie master say?" asks the same fella.

"He just laughed and told him, 'You've got our best caddie.'"
"But Ol' Beebop just snarled back, 'Well if McRae's the best, I'd
hate to see the worst.' That man was in one nasty mood that day."

After another hardy laugh, someone remarks they heard I was
a good golfer in my day. I know from past experience if they've
got to this point in the conversation, time on my tired sore feet is
just about over.

It's always surprised me that I don't know many farmers who
golf. Farmers certainly got the land, all they need's a club and a few
balls and they could practice every day.

"Don't have the time for it," Grandpa snapped at me just after I
started to caddy.

"But you'd be *good*, Grandpa!"

He looked at me, plain annoyed. "Now I don't mind you banging
around that ball, long as you do it on your own time. Make sure
your chores are done first."

I smiled ear-to-ear. My chores *were* done so I headed for the barn.
Found a saw and a hatchet and made my way to the woods to hunt
for just the right blackjack...blackjack's a kinda oak tree...I was after
one with a curved root. About half hour later I stumbled across

one...no, I mean it...fell right over the damn thing...wasn't much taller than me. "Perfect," I thought. Well I worked at that root for about an hour before it finally gave way – brought my prize back to the barn and after much cutting and sanding, the root finally took the shape of a driver head. Its hardness was just a shade less than aged persimmon. I cut the tree to fit my height and wrapped masking tape around skinny trunk to form a grip.

Now Dad caddied at Pinehurst for thirty-five years, but he never was much of a golfer...don't think he really had the interest. But when I caddied, I studied golfers and how they swung the club. Though I didn't know much about the game, it was easy to pick and see what to do and what *not* to do when swinging a golf club.

I heard Miller Barber once owned a driving range just so he could hit balls every day. When he eventually joined the tour, he sought instruction from any pro who'd volunteer some. I figured that's how I'd learn the game, too. Lacey Rush owned a driving range not far from me in Taylortown and we'd hit balls at night. The range included a couple of sand holes and makeshift greens made of sand where we actually could play a game. They were just 9-iron length, so they were good for practicing chips and pitches too. All those fine golfers I caddied for served as my instructors. Take the club back low and long as you can. Break the right arm but keep that left arm *straight*...start bringing the club down while driving with the left leg. Let the wrists and hands come square into the ball. Finish high on the left side. I tried to hit a bunch of old balls that way every day – repeating and repeating the swing over and over until it come natural to me. I beat that blackjack into the ground until my hands ached so hard I could hardly hold the club. Then I borrowed a 5-iron and did the same with it...then a 7...an 8...and finally a 9.

One day when I was caddying for Jim Hunter, he surprised me on the 12th tee.

"Okay, Willie," he said, handing back his driver. "It's *your* turn."

"What, suh?" I replied, stunned. I was a few weeks away from just my eleventh birthday but I already knew blacks weren't allowed to play on Number 2 except during the Caddie Tournament.

"It's okay. Here, *take it*," he insisted, pushing the club into my hands.

My eyes musta been the size of saucers as I stared at that driver.

"Here's a tee and ball," he went on. "Now step up and pound one."

That day I actually hit *fifteen* balls off the 11th tee. We weren't holding up nobody...so nobody cared...seemed like it was just the two of us for miles around. Mr. Hunter was a terrific guy and great motivator. We cleaned out his bag of golf balls so it took a while to collect them all. But when I was retrieving them I couldn't help but notice I hit them all pretty straight...and to my surprise...*l-o-n-g*. I'd played other sports – like baseball and football – but none of them ever took hold of me like golf. Standing on that tee, I felt the blood course my veins so hard it seemed like it poured right down the shaft of that club. Shot after shot, I felt more comfortable...was just me and the club like we was one...right then and there I knew I was born to golf. Always being around golf and golf courses as much as I was, it had become part of me just like my heart and soul.

Well my reputation as a kid who could hit a golf ball spread pretty fast and before long other golfers started letting me drive a couple of balls. Mr. Eddie Nesbitt — he owned a soda company in Philadelphia — even let me hit a couple on the 1st tee of Number 2 right in front of a small band of players. A few years later Richard Tufts bought me a set of MacGregor clubs and said, "Make me proud." So that's what I set out to do.

Anyone could play at Fort Bragg and there was a group of caddies who drove to the base and played twice a week. When I was fifteen, the group — there was eight of them and all older than me — had an opening so they invited me to play. Problem was, they weren't just all older than me, they all resented my close relationship to Mr. Tufts too. They wanted me to play with them so they could take my money. Well...that was their plan, anyway...

By then caddies were making $30 to $35 a week so the game stakes were stiff: the loser paid $5 to each of the other seven players. I was playing good...or so I thought...finished the front 9 with a 38.

"Pay up, McRae," Fletcher Gaines ordered.

"But we gotta play nine holes yet," I answered.

The others laughed...Fletcher flashed me his full set of teeth. "We pay after each 9 and we'll be happy to take your money again after 18."

He had me by about 16 years and even more pounds, so what could I do? What an initiation...*out $35!* I knew right then and there I couldn't afford to lose no more.

"I know I can beat you guys," I blurted. I knew I musta sounded like a sour grapes young kid but I was mad and the thing was, I knew I really could.

"Then *prove* it," Lee Stancie challenged me.

I parred the 10th and drove the 295-yard par 4, 11th. After two-putting that hole, I birdied the 12th and 14th...made me three under for nine. The rest of my foursome was seething and word of my success spread to the rest of our group on up ahead. Now they were all mad at me...I didn't care...their anger just pushed me to do that much better. *Think you're gonna take **my** money? I'll just see about that...*Pars on the next three holes positioned me to be the big winner this side.

"We're pressing you, McRae," Fletcher announced on the 18th tee...no teeth showing now.

I could lose it all if I lost the press and would go home out $35.

"I don't think — "

"We don't care what you think," he cut me off. *"We're pressing."*

O-k-a-a-a-y...The 18th was a long par 5 that ran along Highway 87. Longer than the others, I knew if I stayed away from the out-of-bounds on the right I could reach the green in two. I *did*...and I was the *only* one who did. Two putts later I collected $105 from the other seven. I'd survived my initiation, and became a regular in the twice-a-week trips to Fort Bragg.

"You may be doing pretty good out *here*," Fletcher Gaines told me after a match one day. "But wait until I get you in the caddie tournament coming up."

Being the cocky 15-year-old brat I was, I just smiled and said, "Bring your best."

Playing from the white tees on Number 2, Fletcher and me both shot 75 in the next Caddie Tournament...we beat the field but still had to square off in a nine-hole playoff. The tournament featured some pretty respectable golf so when it got around that Fletcher and me tied with 75s, a crowd of caddies and Pinehurst members alike collected to see the playoff. When I think back on it now, I know what I needed was someone who had my back...someone who'd give me some words of encouragement when I needed them...someone who believed in me. But I had Dad on my bag and he wasn't much use. He was too busy sneaking swigs of vodka from a flask he'd stowed in my golf bag, to pay much attention to anything else.

Well Fletcher ended up thumping me bad that afternoon. I shot one of my worst scores ever – 43 – to his steady-as-a-rock 38. Guess he was good about it but he never let me forget it neither. It'd be twelve years before we'd be pitted against each other like that again.

I remember Dad and me sitting under our *Tree of Knowledge* the night before that next tournament.

"Sorry, son," he said sipping at his vodka. "I can lug your bag tomorrow, Willie, but I know I'm not worth a damn to you out there. Just wish I could do better for you."

I tried to imagine how he musta felt when he drove his Jeep over that German mine during the war...but the notion was so foreign to me...just couldn't altogether get my mind around it. "Don't worry about it none...I know why you need to drink," was all I could manage to tell him.

The next day I bought him another fifth of Smirnoff. I stuffed it in my golf bag and we made our way to the golf course. That year the Caddie Tournament was on Pinehurst Number 3. And sure enough when the dust settled in the end, Fletcher and me stood tied again. We both managed to shoot 74 over the short, but diabolical course, and then headed for the 1st tee for another dreaded shoot-out...and this time...sudden death.

The 1st hole on that course is a short par 4 with a large tree stuck right in the middle of the fairway...guess it's supposed to make the hole a little more interesting. I pulled a 3-wood...that left me an easy wedge to the green. Ever confident, Fletcher Gaines stepped up to his shorter wedge shot, but caught it thin. *Hadn't expected that one*...and could tell by the way that smile ran away from Fletcher's face, he didn't neither. Never before or since have I ever seen a smile leave someone's face so fast. There he was, stuck out there a *mile* from the pin. Well ol' Fletcher couldn't manage any better than a three-putt. *The winner's take was mine.* I'd waited twelve painful long years for this moment so believe you me, I relished every last bit of it.

Dad was ecstatic and gave a hole-by-hole recount all the way home. I'd won $75 and the first thing I bought was another fifth for my dad. As we sat under our *Tree of Knowledge* late that afternoon, I asked him, "Don't you think you've had enough to drink?"

But he just looked at me with glassy eyes and flashed me a big wet smile. "Son," he said, "There's no use building a fire just to put it out."

I just shook my head, smiled back and handed him the rest of the money.

"Now wait," he protested. *"What are you doing?"*

"It's for you and mom," I said. "Beating Fletcher was all I wanted. The money's yours."

Now Dad was well in the wind by time we made it into the house that evening, but he still managed to tell mom, "Our son gave me all his winnings, Emma, and I'm giving you $50 of it."

Well it seemed like our whole house just brimmed with happiness that night. My parents shared a right fine time...hadn't seen them together like that in long, long a while...and I was glad I could give them that moment.

My Time with Sugar Ray

Now you'll remember, years before, I'd played on the golf teams at Fort Jackson and Fort Dix. My friend, Major James had made sure I followed him to Fort Dix and we used to team up regular to play against a sergeant and a full-bird colonel. We played against them five or six times and each time left them both crying like babies. They knew we were better than they were so it musta been the challenge — you know — the burning desire to thump us just once — that kept bringing them back for more.

The sergeant played a pretty good game, but he couldn't putt good as me. After they lost that last time, the sergeant pulled me aside and asked, "Why don't *we* become partners for a while?"

"Fine by me," I answered.

Now I still played some with Major James but the sergeant and me started playing ourselves around the club...won most of the time too. Sometimes we even played head-to-head, but we kept it friendly.

Can't recall him *ever* beating me, but I knew his son could. That sergeant's name was Earl Woods...he called his son *Tiger*.

As a member of the Fort Dix golf team, I got to play several New York courses including the famous Beth Page Black, site of past and future U.S. Opens. Now the pro there, Zeke Ross, took a genuine liking to me. At the time he was giving lessons to Sugar Ray Robinson, the middle-weight boxing champ. Sugar Ray, turns out, needed a golfing partner to take on a couple of high rollers who picked the numbers and Zeke thought I should meet the boxer at his nightclub in New York City to discuss the option. "You'll be free on the house," he told me, but when I showed up at the front door with some friends, a bouncer about twice my size blocked our entry.

"Hi, I'm Willie McRae. I'm here looking for Sugar Ray," I said.

"Right, but you gotta to pay to get in," the stone-faced man grunted, his arms folded.

I looked at my friends. This wasn't the way it was supposed to be. "Maybe if you could get Sugar Ray to the door," I coaxed with a smile.

"Wait here," grumbled the man. He returned shortly after with the champ who welcomed us with open arms. "Willie McRae," he beamed. "Well, it's great to meet you. Zeke told me that you could help me out. Come on in." He looked at the bouncer. "It's okay. He's my new best friend."

Mr. Robinson showed us to a table and ordered the works. The four of us sat talking, eating and laughing for more than an hour.

"...and I'll cover all our expenses," the boxer said after our lengthy discussion. "So...are you in?"

I smiled ear-to-ear. "You bet."

"Good," said Sugar Ray. "I'll get things set up and call you."

This was a big deal. No, I mean it...a *really big deal.* Playing against these guys would only cost me gas money to drive back and forth to the course...and when I thought about the money we could win...*wow!* I wanted to be sure I was ready, so the next day I headed to Orchard Hills Golf Course outside Hackensack, New Jersey to practice. But when I got there, I ran into Sugar Ray.

"What are *you* doing here?" he asked me excitedly.

"Just came by to hit a little," I answered.

"Can you believe it?!" The champ sounded like he was in overdrive he was so excited. "Those men I was telling you about last night...well they're here and they want to play."

*"*What...*now?"*

"Yeah, *right now*...can you do it?"

I wasn't exactly short on time so I said, "Why not?"

Herbert Robinson — no relation to the boxer — and his friend Pat Suggs, were two big burly guys who thought they played like Jack Nicklaus. Both men extended their hands...I saw the Rolexes on their wrists and knew their pockets ran deep...real deep. "Willie McRae. Why you guys look like brothers," Mr. Suggs commented.

"Depending on how he plays," the boxer replied, "we might be."

"Well, if he's no better than you, Sugar Ray," said Mr. Robinson. "He'll be okay."

That comment frosted the champ but good. As we saddled up to the 1st tee, Sugar Ray whispered, "Bet what you want. I'll cover you." *WOW*...He'd already covered my greens fees.

I nodded just before hooking my opening drive dead left in a thicket of trees. Not the most impressive start to say the least, and I remember hearing our opponents chuckling themselves silly as we left the tee. Now maybe it was 'cause I was stiff or maybe it was 'cause of the way I was rushed to start with, but truth is, my game really didn't improve much after that. Coming off the 9th green, I posted a 43. We were down four.

"Sugar Ray, you sure have been having a tough time finding a good partner," Mr. Suggs cracked.

Sugar Ray didn't say nothing...he just glared at *me*. I knew I needed to do something to turn this match around...and *fast*.

"Tell you what," I piped up in challenge. "Give us $500 to our $100 that I'll shoot seven strokes better on the back."

The two men looked at each other in disbelief. *"You ever play this course before?"* asked Mr. Robinson real suspicious like.

I shook my head and said, "No." The men exchanged oozing smiles...they were all but drooling and were all too eager to take that bet. Of course...they did live to regret that decision...I proceeded to flip my front 9 score on the back, 43 to 34. *Boy, were those guys mad!* But even though they fussed and fumed that whole day, they ended up coming back every week for more punishment...and every week we took them for $400 to $500. I lived real fine as a private that last year in the army and the champ was pretty happy too.

When I came home to Pinehurst, I started caddying for John R. Sibley. He owned prize-winning Jersey cows back in his hometown of Spencer, Massachusetts. For four straight summers I served as his chauffeur and drove him back and forth to Massachusetts. Turned out pretty good for me too 'cause every time we were up in New England, Jimmy Tonsall — he owned Lester Hill Country Club — invited me to play his golf course during my free time. He used to visit Mr. Sibley in Pinehurst so him and me had become friends. You know to this day I hold their course record of 64.

Now down the road from the club was a driving range managed by Tom Daley. I had this one warm up exercise...to get my rhythm I used to hit several 3-woods in a row without stopping. Tom spotted me one day and suggested we might make some money at night with this game. I kinda liked that idea so when I came back later and started my warm up, Tom came out of his little driving range shop, gathered up some of his clientele and declared, "I bet Willie McRae here can hit ten balls over two hundred yards without ever pausing. Do I have any takers?"

And he had takers...every night for the next few weeks I would pound out 3-woods, *all* over two hundred yards plus. Betting people, I have found, are kinda funny. Just like with Earl Woods and the full-bird and the number pickers, and these people at the range...same thing...the more they lose...the more their zest to win grows. It's like they can't help themselves...like my dad and his drinking. After about a month, though, we'd run through most of Tom's clientele so fewer and fewer were accepting his nightly wager. But at least, for that one month, the good people of Spencer padded my wallet real nice like.

But around 1960 I developed a bad case of the shanks...just kept hitting shot after shot on the hosel of the club. I know they say a shank is the closest thing to a perfect shot, but anyone who slips into this habit knows it behaves like a downright crippling disease. Got so frustrated and mad I sold my clubs and bought a set of Dunlop clubs. God's own truth...I really did. But like most problems in golf, it went away and fortunately for me, not before I realized that caddying was what I needed to be doing.

Willie (back row, second from right), with his six brothers,
five sisters and mother Emma Lee (front row center)

CHAPTER TWELVE

THE WORLD
GOLF HALL OF FAME

I feel my weight shifting back and forth...one foot to the other...and I'm sure some of them suits must be taking notice. This old man, they must be thinking, looks to be getting real tired. And I am...but even so my mind can't help recalling the many stories that have shaped my life. 'Course it's getting late and I know those suits have been at it since early morning...they're ready to call it a day as well.

But just when I think we're about to wrap up, someone I can't see asks me the one question of all questions. "Willie, how did it feel to be inducted into the World Golf Hall of Fame?"

What a thrill that was...I tell you true, it was the highlight of my career and I have to personally thank the leaders of Pinehurst at the time, Bob Dedman Sr. and Pat Corso, for that. I know they played a big part in making it happen.

But Pat Corso did something real special that affected caddies not just in Pinehurst, but everywhere. Up until the late '90s, caddies just showed up to work. There was no organization, no formal training, no nothing. They were left to their own devices, so to speak.

Some caddies took pride in their work and done a good job. But now others simply went through the motions and some of those motions ended up alienating the golfers they caddied for. Our new management not only brought organization and training to the caddie ranks, but went one major step further. They created the Pinehurst Caddie Hall of Fame to recognize exceptional caddies. This was the first time caddies were officially recognized for being an important part of golf. This was a big deal 'cause it made you feel like you counted and that you were appreciated for what you did. It was this recognition that gave us incentive to improve our performance. Guess you could say it bumped us all up a notch. I was one of the fortunate ones to make it into the first inaugural class. Nine of my long-time buddies did too. To this day pictures of Hardrock Robinson, Robert Stafford, Jimmy Steed, Hilton Rogers, Fletcher Gaines, hang among others in the hallway of the Pinehurst Resort Club.

But this local recognition turned out to be just the beginning for me...was kinda like a door opening wide to new possibilities.

One day out of the blue, Jimmy Smith, our caddie master, got a call from the World Golf Hall of Fame in St. Augustine, Florida. They wanted him to nominate one caddie from Pinehurst. Now there were a number of good men working the courses with me so I was truly grateful Jimmy Smith picked me. But now wouldn't you just know it, the day I was supposed to leave for Florida, I had to caddy 36 holes too. I was dead tired by the time I made it home, but the thought of being inducted into the World Golf Hall of Fame sure 'nough had my adrenaline pumping too. So my wife Hattie of these many recent years and me piled into the car and hardly even noticed driving all night. We made it to St. Augustine by four in the morning. I tell you true that drive was worth the effort. Yes, suh. We got treated just like royalty...had big hotel rooms and even a limousine to haul us around. Best of all they paid for the whole thing. It was truly a time to remember.

A small bunch of caddies had the honor that year. The hall even hosted a celebrity captain's choice tournament the day before our induction for the standout among us, Bruce Edwards, the legendary caddie for Tom Watson. Bruce was a genuine prince...real likable sort...bless his soul...we lost that poor man way too young to Lou Gehrig's disease.

But I guess it was just meant to be my day on the links. After I smacked a putt from eighty yards off the green to within three feet of the hole, I knew the time was ours. My foursome included a long bomber off the tee. He could park it in the fairway most holes and leave the rest of us with fairly short approach shots. All of us got pretty good with a wedge over the course of that memorable afternoon and we walked away with a sweet win.

By then most of my family had arrived – Brenda, my daughter, Paul, my oldest son and Bentley, my youngest, along with Darick, my grandson. Sure wish my other two boys, Roland and Larry, could have been there, too. Kinda like to think they were somewhere about, waiting to see their father inducted into the Hall of Fame. I'll tell you there's nothing like having family around you in times like these. Sure...receiving that honor was real special...but it was getting to share it with family that made my moment complete. And by family I'm not just talking about my blood. I'm talking about the other caddies and their families, too. I couldn't remember when I'd ever felt such a strong connection between my own family and the career I've loved all these years. Was kinda like we was all one, bonded together by the same love and purpose. The power of that experience was so strong it was like something you could take hold of and feel in your hands.

I was still reflecting on that powerful connection the next morning as I looked over at Hattie while we cruised along in the stretch limousine to the World Golf Hall of Fame.

Then I looked over at the young boy who had hitched a ride with us. He was looking a might unsettled so I told him, "I know you'll be a good caddie someday."

"Maybe, sir," he replied politely. "But I'm real nervous right now."

"How so?"

"I have to give a speech for my father," he told me.

I smiled at Bruce Edward's son. A small chip off the old block, the boy was much like his dad...entertaining, naturally affable and a joy to be with. "You'll do fine," I reassured him...and about an hour later, he did.

At the ceremony I had to say a word or two as well. Was just as nervous as I was during those money matches...maybe more. Standing there waiting on my turn to speak, I thought to myself, "Would be really good to have a coach right about now." Just then he came to me, big as life, Dean Smith, legendary basketball coach of the North Carolina Tarheels. Remembering my times caddying for that great guy got me through those anxious moments before the mic was mine. Funny thing was he musta been thinking about me too 'cause after I was inducted, he wrote to say how proud he was of me...how I deserved this honor. Yes, suh, good man that Dean Smith.

No surprise to me they asked me what I thought it takes to be a good caddie.

"Don't be a bag toter," I quipped. "Bag toter's no better than a cart. Can't ask him nothing 'cause he don't know nothing." I paused, taking in the laughter. Then I reached far back to remember the words of my father. "Show up, keep up and shut up," I shared with the crowd. It was good advice when Dad had told me then and it was good advice now. I know he woulda been right proud and I know he was thanking me for including him in my special moment. And, of course, I couldn't forget Mom. "One last point," I announced. "Mother whiff."

"What's that?" came the predictable question.

The common sense knowledge only a mom can impart.

Four Generations of McRae's:
(from left to right) Willie's son Paul, Willie, Willie's grandson
Darick, and Paul's wife LaRee Sugg McRae with their son
James Thaddeus in the front

CHAPTER THIRTEEN

OTHERS HAVE A WORD

"*Willie you should write a book,*" *comments red tie after I tell them my story about Sugar Ray Robinson.*

"*Thought about it,*" *I reply. "But don't know how much I'd remember or if I'd keep all the names straight.*"

"*Well, you're doing just fine tonight,*" *paisley tie adds.*

"*Owe it all to Pinehurst...and golf,*" *I think about that for a moment. "The two are the same thing you know...Pinehurst kinda defines golf in America.*"

"*Sure, it's been around as long as golf has in this country,*" *offers yellow tie.*

"*Oh, it's more than that,*" *I struggle to explain. "Like tonight... we've talked about lotta famous people who've played Pinehurst, but it seems like everybody's played there over the years. They come from all over the world to play the St. Andrew's of the U.S., and most of them don't have nearly the deep pockets you might expect. Down through the years, all the Tufts wanted Pinehurst to be a family place and somehow it's managed to stay pretty much that way to this day. Sure's been family to me. My son works there, even my grandson.*"

It's getting late...I'm pretty tired by now and the new questions coming at me all seem to mush together...my feet are so sore from standing that they're making it hard for me to think. I'd just like to sit down and enjoy a frosty one. As this thought starts to take over my mind, I hear that all too familiar Charlotte voice from well back in the crowd. "Give the poor man a break," bellows Johnnie Harris. "There're a few people in the room who know this man quite well and can probably tell you more about him that he can himself."

The crowd parts and I see some of my dearest friends alongside Mr. Harris. The moment warms my heart and it pushes me back to remember the sea of friends and acquaintances from days long gone and how they've all enriched my life at Pinehurst.

What a lucky man I been.

Pat Corso

Diamondhead's try at rapid development antagonized local residents more and more. In 1980 the citizens finally got the state to incorporate the Village of Pinehurst. Up until then Diamondhead owned the whole community. But mounting debt and sluggish sales were staggering management same way Sugar Ray Robinson and Carmen Basilio used to beat on one another. So finally in 1984, Diamondhead handed the reigns over to Clubcorp. Clubcorp was owned by Robert Dedman. Mr. Dedman was a remarkable business-man...came to be known as the "Henry Ford of the Club Management Business," since Clubcorp had facilities in cities around the country, plus a bunch of prime golf courses, like the Greenbrier in West Virginia. Mr. Dedman picked Pat Corso to be head of Pinehurst Operations and then Mr. Corso picked the venerable Don Padgett Sr. to run the golf side of the business.

Pinehurst was the jewel in Mr. Dedman's crown – he just loved it...and Pat Corso made sure everything ran perfect. Between the two of them they restored the Carolina Hotel to its original Victorian splendor. Then they purchased and restored the Holly Inn and added the Centennial Course – Course Number 8 – to commemorate "Pinehurst's 100th Birthday." Better still, Don Padgett had exceptional connections in the golf world and managed to attract several key tournaments to the resort. First the USGA sent the 1989 Women's Amateur, and then the PGA brought its Tour Championship in 1991 and 1992. These tournaments paved the way for the U.S. Senior Open two years later and ultimately the 1999 U.S. Open. *That* tournament featured the thrilling comeback by Payne Stewart...to this day, it still ranks as one of the greatest Opens of all time.

Pat Corso Remembers...

Willie and I go back a long way. He hung with me for many a round. In fact, as we came up the 18th on Number 2 one day, he said, "I seen parts of this golf course today I ain't never seen before." But Willie coached me well. Soon after that fateful day, we came to the 8th tee and I was only two over par.

"You can be even on the front if you just birdie the next two holes," he said with an encouraging smile.

Yeah right, I thought, but phenomenally, I did birdie both 8 and 9 registering par for the front side and 78 for the round.

Willie was always on my bag and it gave me pleasure to nominate him to the Pinehurst Hall of Fame. I'm thankful for what Willie did for me; he personified what a caddie should be so when my youngest son, Michael, was ready to play Number 2 at age fourteen, I wanted Willie to be there. I wanted to expose my son not only to the great golf course, but also let him experience the total Number 2 experience, replete with a top-notch caddie like Willie. Donald Ross' creation was meant to be played stepping off the fairways with a good caddie by your side.

As we left the 1st tee that day, I asked my son, "Do you understand what this means?"

Michael glanced at Willie, who winked back at him. "Oh, Dad," my son said. "I surely do."

Little did I know just moments before Willie had asked him a similar question. I'm grateful to both men for letting me glimpse my young son for the first time as a man.

Stewart Taylor

I remember Mr. Taylor far back as the mid '60s, when he shined as an outstanding junior golfer. To this day his cocky swagger has seen him through many a rough spot. He played the Donald Ross Junior Invitational in 1965 and declared that he was gonna shoot a 68. Although he actually inverted that score, the 86 didn't faze him none and he went on to be an accomplished golfer. He played his college golf at the University of South Carolina and is currently the PGA Director of the Eastern Junior Golf Association. Like most golfers worth their salt, Taylor's given back to the community. His tireless teaching is an inspiration to young players and has surely raised the caliber of Sandhill golfers.

Stewart Taylor Remembers...

I have to tell you up upfront that golf was never meant to be played while riding around in a cart. It was meant to be played while walking side-by-side with a caddie, playing a game and more...taking in the surroundings almost like a spiritual event. And if you're ever lucky enough to have Willie by your side, you get to listen to the history of Pinehurst come alive.

Best of all he helped immensely in getting me through the tough rounds. He certainly helped me win the Pinehurst Pro-Am Tournament back in 1979, no doubt about it. When you find a good caddie, you keep him like a key club in your bag. Of course Willie was much more than that to me.

We would have conversations on the course like this...

Willie: "The putt's going to the right two inches."

Me: "Doesn't look like it's going right."

And I would get that "are you questioning me" look.

Willie: "Right, two inches."

Or...

Willie: "It's 182 yards to the hole."

Me: "Now how do you know it's 182 yards exactly?

I would get that look from him again and occasionally a "trust me."

Willie was always right on the button, both in the fairways and on the greens. And when I trusted him, I would prove him right. Donald Ross made his upside-down greens to test iron play. You have to hit your approach shots to a relatively small section of the greens or they will slip off the precipitous sides. But did the incredible Ross ever dream that a caddie like Willie would come along and simplify the golfer's strategy the way he does? Willie takes the guess work out of navigating Number 2.

I believe you have to be either really smart or really dumb to play the game of golf, because if you're somewhere in the middle, you're in trouble. Having a good caddie helps you around that problem, especially when the caddie, like Willie, is also a superlative player. The relationship a golfer has with his caddie is also special. For four hours you're locked in the challenge of mastering tough terrain. But at the end of the day that caddie lets you loose. What other relationships are that unique?

Still that's the kind of relationship you want to have with your caddie, and while I certainly consider Willie a friend, I'm glad through the years we've had that special bond.

Tom Stewart

Mr. Stewart's a legend in the sport of golf. He's an author and a life member of the Professional Golf Association. For years he's owned one of the most cherished golf landmarks, *Old Sport Gallery*, a real castle of golf memorabilia in downtown Pinehurst. It features priceless photographs and artifacts, along with an impressive collection of books written by some of the richest voices in golf history. His shop's so famous it's listed as one of the top 50 places, outside of courses that is, that every golfer should visit.

Tom Stewart Remembers...

Each day that I saw Willie at the local post office, I knew I would be uplifted. His work with prisoners to scratch players made each person better off through his interaction. He's always had an amazing ability to be both humble and self-confident. I'm not sure how a man comes by that...just the sum of his experiences, I guess. Whichever, he is an authentic modern man. Willie McRae is a character with character and I'm better off for having known him.

Tom Herndon

Mr. Herndon is one in a long list of players I've developed friendships with over the years...friendships that go beyond the usual caddie-golfer relationship. Tom and me linked up for the first time little more than a decade ago. Since then we've played several rounds together each year. He hails from Maryland but makes the trip to Pinehurst every year, just like many of my friends do, and I'm grateful to him and all the rest of them for doing so.

Tom Herndon Remembers...

I had never played golf with a caddie before. I checked into the pro shop of Course Number 8 shortly before 7a.m.

"How does this caddie service work?" I asked like a real rookie.

The pro just smiled and said. "You'll find out. You're caddie is Willie McRae and he's been waiting for you since 6:00."

That was a bit intimidating, but had I known I was about to meet a golf legend, I probably wouldn't have had the legs to complete the round that day.

"Call me Willie," he announced when I shook his hand. Little

did I know as I warmed up on the practice green and range that all the while, Willie had placed a watchful eye on my putting and hitting routines.

My foursome wanted to play from the gold tees that day and to me that meant taking out the big stick for every par 4. But when Willie handed me a 3-wood on the 1st tee, I snapped, "Willie, I need the driver."

"No ya don't, Tom," Willie said leaving no room for discussion. "Draw it back a bit 'n it'll roll right down the hill."

At that moment I thought having a caddie was a huge mistake and hoped he wouldn't be so arbitrary for the rest of the round. But after I hit the 3-wood of my life, my edge softened.

"Golf shot," was all Willie said.

I would soon learn the significance of that statement.

My caddie showed no mercy. For my second shot — I was 114 yards from the pin — and said as politely as I could muster, "My pitching wedge, please."

When he handed me my sand wedge, I protested, "I can only hit this eighty or ninety yards.

Willie sniffed and looked offended. "We don't want to be past the hole."

As I set up to the shot, I thought about all the money I'd paid for this round and questioned whether it was worth it. But when the ball carried some twenty yards farther than I thought it would, I shrugged and smiled as I heard Willie say, "Golf shot, but I told you to keep it below the hole."

On the green I told Willie I was going to read the putt, which I did from behind it, below the hole and both sides. "A fifteen-footer," I declared. "Two-foot break, left to right."

Without a word Willie walked six feet left of my ball mark and pointed to a repaired divot on the green. "Roll it right next to this divot 'n play it like a ten-footer. Fifteen is way too hard."

I really didn't see that read and knew in my heart that if I did what Willie said, the ball wouldn't come near the hole. His call ran counter to everything I'd seen or experienced in golf. My mind was spinning with hesitation but for some fortunate reason I listened to my caddie. Somehow the ball rolled near that divot and started bending to the right...then farther right...farther still like the ball was truly seeking the hole. My foursome erupted when it rattled in the cup and I barely heard Willie remark, "Golf shot."

As we approached the 2nd tee, I conceded almost apologetically, "Thanks Willie. I'll never question your advice again."

Since then, Willie and I have played many times together. He even coached me to a birdie on the ridiculously hard hole 5 on Number 2, as well as giving me the exact read on hole 4 in tournament play.

But I will best remember Willie for the man he is...his special treatment of people, his respect for the game...a true gentleman. Golf history is lucky to have him and I'm proud to know him.

He may be missing a thumb from a work-related accident long ago, but I've seen him nail one-hand wedges consistently to within 10 feet of the hole. That's just the way of Willie McRae.

Don Padgett II

Mr. Padgett, son of the man who brought tournament golf to Pinehurst, is the resort's president and a great golfer in his own right. Before following in his father's footsteps at our fabled resort, Don did a number of special things at Firestone Country Club in Akron, Ohio.

I owe a lot to him. Because of my age, Don made the controversial decision to let me ride a golf cart on the fairways of Number 2...no one else is allowed to do that without special permission. That thoughtfulness allowed me to continue my career and for that, I'm deeply grateful.

Don approached. I could almost see his parents, one on each side of him, and remembered how much Don Sr. liked the caddies and our Pinehurst Caddie Hall of Fame. His wife, Joanne, sent me the nicest note when I was inducted into the World Hall...I recall how she made me smile when she told of her husband's caddying days. He used to go to the backdoor of the clubhouse after looping double and pay 5 cents for two chicken wings. Imagine that...great man like Mr. Padgett getting his start caddying. Just goes to show how great a caddy can become.

Don Padgett II Remembers...

People at St. Andrews, the home of golf, say that the spirit of the sport rests there at the royal and ancient club and Pinehurst. I believe that, too, and Willie McRae carries that spirit with him. He embodies Pinehurst and fortunately I believe he has passed that on to me. And members and guests who get to spend time with him get touched by the Pinehurst spirit as well.

Willie may be long in the tooth, but he's also young at heart. That's been a tad hard for his son, Paul, and grandson, Darick, to grasp. They've challenged us at golf and would like nothing better to get into our wallets.

"We have enough money to play you guys," Paul announced last year and Darick prematurely boasted about victory that sadly existed only in his mind. I've never shied from a match and neither has Willie. We took on the young bucks and as fate would have it, we won rather handily. Willie got their money and we both got bragging rights.

When Darick dared to ask me why his grandfather had special privileges on Number 2, I told him, "When you're in the World Golf Hall of Fame, come see me about riding those fairways."

Paul McRae

Now where did he come from? That's my son, Paul, coming through the crowd. Boy, what great times we had. I had such joy watching him and my other kids grow up. Paul's always had that way about him...you know...real easy and fun to be around. He's polite but now he's a constant kidder too. And never bragged 'bout his rich athletic talent neither. No...always wore it real quiet like even though he was a high school star in baseball, basketball and football. Paul never had much time for golf as a youngster no matter how much I tried to make him. It was only after college and a stint in the army that he decided to try golf. And when he finally did, he threw himself into the game with full out passion. In fact, making up for lost time, he married Laree. A good golfer as well, she fit perfectly into the McRae family. She actually sunk the last putt that gave the UCLA Bruins a national championship a few years back. I'm so glad he's here.

Paul McRae Remembers...

"I've got to set the record straight about this golf match you just heard about," he starts. Uh oh, I know the mistake he's about to make. *"Darick and I played against Mr. Padgett and Dad on Willie's birthday. Now I'm not saying we thr-..."* he shrugs... *"We backed off a bit."*

I can't resist and break in. *"Tell it true, son. When you and Darick wouldn't concede Mr. Padgett that eleven-inch putt on the first green, you made him mad.*

"More like a five-footer," is his lame response.

I ignore it. *"And what did Mr. Padgett do after that?"*

Paul confesses, *"Hit fairways and greens all day."* I smile content and let him go on. *"Those are the kind of moments I remember sharing with Dad. He tried to get me into the game early, but it didn't take. When I was barely five, he set tin cans into holes in the back yard...nine of them. We'd putt at those holes till dark. Other sports called me then, but when golf became a priority, I reached back to all Dad had taught me...and it was plenty. After six months of pounding balls on the range, I broke 85 my first time out and not long after I became a professional. And that's when my father went from being Dad to being both a coach and a competitor."*

Paul chuckles and scratches his head. *"Dad had a funny way of* coaching me. Once when I was trying to qualify for the U.S. Open, he told me the night before the crucial round, 'Son, no offense, but you still can't putt a lick.' Sure enough, next day with Dad on the bag showing me the right lines on every green, the flat stick failed me. But then there was the time, again when Dad was caddying for me on Number 2. I was in and out of trouble most of the front nine." Paul glances my way and I recall the round like it happened yesterday.

"This guy Track and I were getting thumped by John Curtis and Jim Frye. On the 10th tee Dad whispers, 'We're down $100.' 'Down,' I say, 'but we're not betting anybody.' 'Sure are,' Dad snaps. 'I've got a wager with their caddie and it's going the wrong way every hole. You best pick it up, Son.' Well, I couldn't let Dad down or there'd be hell to pay...his urgent words hit me like a kick in the butt and spurred me to shoot 32 on the back side, putting money in his wallet instead of his having to shovel it out."

"I could tell a hundred stories like those," Paul says, recalling some he would never tell. "The to and fro between Dad and me has always come easy." He glances my way and we share a moment lost on many in the crowded room.

"Willie, your competitor?" comes from somewhere in the throng. "How so?"

Paul laughs and I know what's coming next. "Once I gave a lesson to a gentleman who Dad was about to caddy for," he begins. "When Dad met the man on the first tee, he told him, 'Now forget everything you think you were just taught.'"

The room erupts in laughter. I couldn't have told the story any better.

"Yes, from time to time Dad still reminds me who's on first," he goes on. "A few years back, he and I played Number 2 together. I played a heck of a round that day and could've sworn I'd beaten him. To this day I think the scorecard lied. It said we tied...66 a piece. I told him, 'Damn, I thought I got you.' His smile was sublime as he replied, 'You didn't teach me, Son. I taught you."

AFTERWORD

I'm about to say, "That's it," 'cause my legs can't hardly take no more when I hear his voice from way back in the crowd surrounding me. I'd know that voice anywhere, heard it a thousand times and it's always brought pleasure to my ears. Over the years I've thoroughly enjoyed caddying for that man...and not just for the big tips he stuffs my pockets with neither. No suh! It's more how I appreciate such a powerful man treating me like a regular guy...well, I just enjoy his company.

"Ladies and gentlemen," Johnnie Harris says in a voice that quiets the room. "I think it's time we give this poor man a well-deserved rest." He begins to head my way, threading his way through the crowd. People separate like they should to let him through. Some say he owns half of Charlotte, North Carolina, but you've never heard it from him. Before he reaches me, he starts, "Willie and I go way back and tonight wouldn't be complete if I didn't have a say."

He gets to where I'm standin' and wraps an arm around my shoulders. The last time I caddied for him, his good friend, Arnold Palmer, strode down the fairways with us step for step. Johnnie starts at the beginning, how he got hurt playin' lacrosse at college and turned to golf. Soon after, he found his way to Pinehurst where we linked up for the first time in the early '70s. Now everybody knows Johnnie Harris sure do like his bacon for breakfast so when him and Macon Moye played golf, they kinda got a team name slapped on 'em. "They called us Macon and Bacon, but we weren't nearly as tough on the course as we sounded," Johnnie confides. He tells story after story and I'm in each one of 'em. He coulda gone on all night I reckon, but as he winds down on another, he sees in my eyes that I'm fadin' fast.

"I'd birdied hole two of Number 2," Johnnie relates, "and actually eagled Number 5, one of the best par 4s out there. Proud as I can be, we marched to the sixth hole and I said to Willie, 'How 'bout that?'" Never cracked a smile, just as matter-of-fact as he could be, he says, 'That's one way to be even after five.' " Laughter rolls over the crowd again, and I think back on that moment. He got it right. Yes, suh. That's exactly what Johnnie was. Even after five.

He looks into my tired eyes. "Willie's never met anyone who stays a stranger for very long," Johnnie tells the crowd without looking at them. It's almost like it's just me and Johnnie Harris filling that great room by ourselves. "I remember one time there were four of us...a friend of mine and two foreigners...playing Number 2. Boy, were those two guys feeling uncomfortable. We could barely get a word out of either one of them for the first few holes. But Willie saw the problem right off...knew how to fix it, too." Johnnie smiles at me and I know what he's 'bout to say. "He just lit us up with jokes and banter plenty for eighteen holes. By the *time we were done, all four of us were friends...four guys playing golf with caddies...everyone the same."*

I take a long look at my friend as the smile broadens on his face. "Willie, actually you can't caddy a lick," he closes. "But I sure do enjoy your company."